SMØRREBRØD

SCANDINAVIAN OPEN SANDWICHES

SMØRREBRØD

SCANDINAVIAN OPEN SANDWICHES

MORE THAN 50 RECIPES, FROM TRADITIONAL TO MODERN

BRONTË AURELL

PHOTOGRAPHY BY PETER CASSIDY

RYLAND PETERS & SMALL
LONDON • NEW YORK

Senior Designer Megan Smith

Editorial Director Julia Charles

Editor Kate Reeves-Brown

Head of Production
  Patricia Harrington

Creative Director
  Leslie Harrington

Food Stylist Kathy Kordalis

Prop Stylist Tony Hutchinson

Indexer Hilary Bird

First published in 2025 by
Ryland Peters & Small
20–21 Jockey's Fields, London
WC1R 4BW
and
1452 Davis Bugg Road
Warrenton, NC 27589

10 9 8 7 6 5 4 3 2 1

Text © Brontë Aurell 2025
Design and photography
© Ryland Peters & Small 2025
(Image on page 109 © Peter Cassidy)

Printed in China.

ISBN: 978-1-78879-645-3

A CIP record for this book is available
from the British Library.

US Library of Congress cataloging-in-
Publication Data has been applied for.

NOTES

· All spoon measurements are level
unless otherwise specified.

· All eggs are medium (UK) or large (US),
unless specified as large, in which case
US extra-large should be used. Uncooked
or partially cooked eggs should not be
served to the very old, frail, young
children, pregnant women or those
with compromised immune systems.

· When a recipe calls for cling film/
plastic wrap, you can substitute for
beeswax wraps, silicone stretch lids
or compostable baking paper for
greater sustainability.

· When a recipe calls for the grated
zest of citrus fruit, buy unwaxed fruit
and wash well before using.

· Ovens should be preheated to the
specified temperatures. If using a fan-
assisted oven, adjust temperatures
according to the manufacturer's
instructions.

· Each recipe is for 2 open sandwiches,
which is enough for a light lunch for
2 people. Most of the open sandwiches
can also be arranged over 4 smaller
pieces of bread, so if you are preparing
a spread for more people, choose
3–4 recipes depending on how many
you are serving.

CONTENTS

INTRODUCTION

Writing a book called *Smørrebrød* has long been a dream. Since emigrating from Denmark, I have spent almost two decades running our London café and food business, serving open sandwiches and other good food from Scandinavia. At our café we don't always stick to everything traditional in our interpretation of *smørrebrød*; we focus on taste and what is good and seasonal, rather than how our parents and grandparents did things.

Our team has worked together to build on Danish, Swedish and Norwegian roots and heritage, what our customers like to eat, what is popular across Scandinavia and how *smørrebrød* culture is continuously developing in Denmark. We focus on good ingredients, taste and making sure we build on the great ideas of traditional *smørrebrød*, putting our own stamp on it. At our place, and in this book, you will find our favourite recipes, from the traditional to more modern interpretations.

Do use our recipes as inspiration to create your own delicious open sandwiches. If you don't have a particular fresh herb, use one you have that works in flavour. Don't have the right kind of pickles? Use something similar. Can't be bothered to make your own crispy onions? Just use store bought. Make the open sandwiches your own – and eat what you love. The perfect open sandwich is one that tastes great, looks great and makes you feel happy when you eat it.

We hope you enjoy our book.

See you soon in our café,

Brontë

Brontë, Jonas and the rest of the ScandiKitchen team x

A BRIEF HISTORY OF SMØRREBRØD

Smørrebrød is a Danish word, derived from the words *smør(re)* (butter or to spread [v]) and *brød* (bread). In Norway, it's *smørbrød*, while in Sweden, you might say *smörrebröd* (referring to the Danish version) or *smörgås*, meaning a piece of bread with toppings.

Smørrebrød became very popular in Denmark in the late 1800s – first, as simple farmer's lunchtime food, and later as a popular decorated lunch dish served in all the fancy places. Nevertheless, the open sandwich – essentially just a piece of bread with toppings – has been around for centuries before this. A slab of bread with toppings used to be called *trenchers* in Middle Age England (before The Earl of Sandwich decided in 1762 that this was inconvenient and added a slice on top so that he could eat it with his hands). Open sandwiches are *tartines* in France, *bruschetta* in Italy and *butterbrot* in Germany. In fact many countries have their own version of the open

sandwich. The Danes, however, have made *smørrebrød* their own and it is a must to sample a few speciality eateries when visiting Denmark.

There are several places in Copenhagen that are credited with having elevated *smørrebrød* into popularity – the currently closed Davidsen restaurant had no fewer than 110 different kinds on their menu. However, you usually find the same 20 or so toppings appearing over and over again on the menus of the most traditional eateries.

After a period of slightly falling out of favour, in recent decades *smørrebrød* has had a huge rise in popularity and now once again appear in trendy cafés and restaurants as the star dishes. This time around, people expect new ideas, new toppings and influences from around the world – including plenty of vegan and vegetarian options. The tradition is still strong but nowadays more so by focusing on the quality of the ingredients, rather than questioning if it is traditional to have herring with beetroot or not. *Smørrebrød* has evolved – and is firmly the Danes' favourite food.

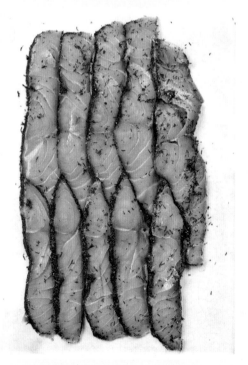

ETIQUETTE

As with all things traditional, there are rules. Some of these rules are logical, and some less so. Most are not written down, which makes it hard for anyone to learn what those rules are. Many are there because that's just the way it has always been done.

The first point – and this rule is actually important – unless you are eating an open sandwich specifically made for hand-delivery (*håndmad* or *snitter*), assume you should use a knife and fork to eat it. It's a safe bet that if you are seated at someone's house or at a café and you are served open sandwiches, cutlery should be used, not your hands.

Sometimes, you may be either serving multiple open sandwiches or enjoying a bit of a feast at someone's house, either with a pre-made selection of open sandwiches or as part of a *koldt bord* (cold table – the Danish version of a Swedish smörgåsbord, where you make your own open sandwiches as you enjoy the meal), if so, then the toppings should be eaten in a certain order:

HERRING – this is **always** eaten first, and most often on a different plate. This is because herring has a very strong taste and using the same plate may 'stain' the rest of the open sandwiches with herring brine, which is not so nice.

Along with the herring, a shot of **cold aquavit** is often served – it complements the pickled fish in taste. You can find an easy recipe for making an aquavit-style spirit at home on page 12. It's an old-school practice that aquavit needs to be kept in the freezer – this just means you won't taste much of it as you drink it. If you find an aquavit with flavour notes you like, try drinking it just lightly chilled instead.

Next up is **FISH AND SEAFOOD** – such as plaice, prawns or *Skagenröra* (see page 28). This stage often includes eggs, too, for those who do not eat fish or those who like eggs with their prawns or salmon.

Following on from this will be any **MEAT OR VEGGIE** options – and if it is a *koldt bord* (especially at Christmas), this is where any hot dishes would also be served.

Lastly, at the end of a meal, you eat any **CHEESE** *smørrebrød* that may be served.

Traditionally, you don't go back once you have moved on to the next course.

Just as important as the order in which you serve the open sandwiches, are the unspoken rules on what goes with what. These rules are taught to us growing up – and some of these I question every day! I've seen non-Scandinavian friends put remoulade dressing on smoked salmon and gasped in horror – before realizing that actually, it's not that bad and there is no reason we have this rule other than 'that's just the way it is'.

SOME OF THE TOPPING COMBINATIONS THAT WILL MAKE ANY DANE SHUDDER (THIS LIST IS NOT EXHAUSTIVE)

» Remoulade on any fish (except fried breaded fish and fish cakes)

» Herring on white or soft bread – it only goes on rye or crispbread

» Remoulade on cheese, herring or liver pâté

» Crispy onions on smoked salmon, prawns, herring, or in fact fish of *any* kind (try telling that to your local sushi take away that nowadays use crispy onions on everything)

» Pickles on any kind of fish

» Combination of two meats together – such as ham and meatballs (there are a few exceptions)

» Cheese and pâté together

While there will always be combinations that people have learned, taste comes first, so forget the above unless you're trying to impress a table full of Danes. Crispy onions are great on salmon and remoulade is nice on pâté. Some people like herring on soft bread – and why not? It's all about what you like.

SMØRREBRØD STYLES

There is a big difference between the *smørrebrød* a Dane might prepare for lunch at home and the version you see in cafés and restaurants. In the most basic sense, an open sandwich is a piece of buttered bread with some form of topping. The Danish word *pålæg* (*pålægg* in Norway, *pålägg* in Sweden) means any form of topping on bread.

HÅNDMAD – a hand-held open sandwich, meaning a piece of bread with *pålæg* that is quite simply decorated so you can deliver it to your mouth with no need for cutlery. This is the open sandwich kids will have in their packed lunch at school and the one you make as a snack when in a hurry. There's minimal decoration, just mainly sustenance. These are most often no bigger than half a slice of rye bread, about 8 x 5 cm/3¼ x 2 inches.

SNITTER – this means 'cut pieces'. They're a little smaller than a *håndmad*, but with more effort on the decorations so they can be served at parties (but not too much so that guests need to use cutlery to eat them). They're larger than a standard canapé (2–3 bites), so are handy if feeding people at a standing event.

SMØRREBRØD – this is the standard with a good amount of *pålæg*. They are the same size as the bread for the *håndmad*, but because these have much more decoration, they are harder to eat without cutlery. This is the size you get in most lunchtime cafés and when making fancy sandwiches for the family. A good option if you want to make a selection for a beautiful lunch, where people might want to sample 2–4 different kinds each.

HØJTBELAGT – this literally means 'high coverage'. No expense is spared on the ingredients and one full piece is often sufficient for the average lunch (or two, for those with larger appetites). The bread is often a whole slice of bread and the toppings cover it completely – and then some. When making these, height and decoration is paramount, as each one is a piece of show *smørrebrød*. In this book, we most often show this larger version, but most of the recipes can be made using half-sized slices (standard *smørrebrød*).

THE ANATOMY OF AN OPEN SANDWICH

It seems so simple – take a piece of bread, put some stuff on it, and eat it. And this is, of course, true.

How to make an open sandwich look good is the tricky bit though. And not just *look* good, but *taste* good and have all the elements of a nice experience *in every bite*. Think of your open sandwich in layers:

FIRST, YOU NEED THE RIGHT BASE – which should complement your choice of toppings. For example, if you are having a mushy topping, such as avocado, choose bread that has a bit of crust, seed or bite to it – a soft white sandwich bread with mushy avocado isn't going to get your mouth excited.

THE BASE NEEDS A SPREAD – butter is the obvious choice. Flavour the butter if you like, but do make it nice quality. I use proper butter, not spreadable – it is just… nicer. The butter also acts as a fat barrier so the toppings will take longer to soak into your slice of bread. This is handy if making your open sandwiches ahead of time.

ADD THE TOPPINGS – on the more traditional *smørrebrød*, people used to add a leaf of lettuce (again, a barrier to stop any toppings soaking the bread), but you should just add the least wet toppings first. For example, if adding salmon and egg salad (which is mayo based and thus also has a fat barrier), add the egg first, then the beautiful salmon on top. If you did it the other way around, the salmon would wet the bread and the egg mayo wouldn't be as visually attractive as a vibrant piece of smoked salmon.

FINALLY, ADD ADDITIONAL TOPPINGS – every type of *smørrebrød* should hit the taste buds (salt, bitter, sour, sweet and umami) and should provide texture and crunch. In this case, the base of seeded rye bread provides great texture with the seeds and malty flavours against the soft, sweet egg salad – finishing with salty smoked salmon on top. Top this with some lightly pickled red onion, crunchy and flavourful fennel, fresh dill, pea shoots and seasoning to finish.

STEP-BY-STEP CONSTRUCTION
OF YOUR OPEN SANDWICH

1. SPREAD THE BASE WITH BUTTER

*Butter creates a barrier to stop the
toppings soaking into the bread.*

2. ADD THE FIRST TOPPING

*The least wet topping should
go on first.*

3. ADD THE PROTEIN

*Arrange the protein
beautifully on top.*

4. ADD TEXTURE AND CRUNCH

*The final toppings will complete
the open sandwich.*

HOMEMADE AQUAVIT

Aquavit is a flavoured alcoholic spirit to enjoy with your smörgåsbord, especially when eating herring, where it is traditional to enjoy a small shot. Dill, caraway and fennel are common flavourings, but berries or flowers can be used too. Purists would use a base such as Brøndums, but vodka is much easier to get hold of outside Scandinavia – as long as it's a flavourless grain- or potato-based spirit over 37.5% proof, you can make an aquavit-style drink with it.

Aquavit must contain dill and caraway to be considered as such – if not, it's a 'snaps'. Whatever you prefer and enjoy is what you should go for – I've seen far too many people feel that they have to suffer drinking an aquavit they don't enjoy.

For a summer aquavit, choose dill, fennel and maybe even elderflower, keeping it lighter in flavour. For the darker seasons, earthy notes such as coriander seed, caraway, cinnamon and cloves, or even allspice, work well.

The general rule is that fresh herbs need only 2–3 days steeping, but dried seeds and barks need several weeks for full flavours to develop. You can add the dried bits first and then the fresh notes at the end of the maturing.

SUMMER AQUAVIT

a bunch of dill
1 teaspoon dill seed
1 teaspoon white sugar
350 ml/1½ cups vodka,
    plus extra to taste

large Kilner/Mason jar, sterilized
paper coffee filter and funnel
glass bottle, sterilized

MAKES 350 ML/1½ CUPS

Blanch the bunch of dill in boiling water for a few seconds, then shake dry and add to the jar (I would always blanch fresh herbs before adding as it gives a stronger taste).

Add the dill seed and sugar, then top up with the vodka and stir. Seal the jar and leave for 4–5 days at room temperature.

Strain through the coffee filter to remove the dill. Decant into the bottle and keep for another month before topping up with more vodka to taste.

Serve slightly chilled in shot glasses.

WINTER AQUAVIT

5 cardamom pods
1 cinnamon stick
8–10 whole cloves
1 teaspoon caraway seeds
½ vanilla pod/bean (used is fine
    – the pod will still have flavour)
1 teaspoon white sugar
1 tablespoon runny honey
350 ml/1½ cups vodka,
    plus extra to taste

large Kilner/Mason jar, sterilized
paper coffee filter and funnel
glass bottle, sterilized

MAKES 350 ML/1½ CUPS

Put the cardamom pods, cinnamon stick, cloves, caraway seeds and vanilla in the jar.

Add the sugar and honey, then top up with vodka and stir. Seal the jar and leave at room temperature for at least 3 weeks.

Strain through the coffee filter to remove the spices. Decant into the bottle and top up with vodka to taste.

Serve slightly chilled in shot glasses.

FISH & SEAFOOD

GRAVAD LAX
DILL-CURED SALMON

*If there is one type of salmon that Swedes love more than any other it has to be
gravad lax, or cured salmon. The cure most often uses dill – and the final result
is fragrant and delicious. At the café, we add new potatoes as a base for a filling
open sandwich, making it more of a satisfying lunch.*

salted butter, for spreading

2 slices of rye bread, or 4
smaller slices (white bread
also works well for this one,
as does Swedish flat bread)

100 g/3½ oz. new potatoes,
cooked, cooled and cut into
bite-sized pieces

4–5 tablespoons Dill & Mustard
Dressing (see right)

115 g/4 oz. Dill-cured Salmon
(see page 124) or store-
bought sliced cured salmon

4 long thin slices of cucumber

2–3 heaped tablespoons cream
cheese

2 tablespoons capers

4–8 pickled cherry tomato
halves (see Cherry Tomato
Quickle, page 114)

freshly ground black pepper

dill sprigs, to garnish

DILL & MUSTARD DRESSING

2 tablespoons Swedish
mustard (I like Slotts Skånsk
Senap – but if you can't get
Swedish, go for a good
grainy mustard)

4 tablespoons finely chopped
dill

1 tablespoon white wine
vinegar

1 teaspoon sugar (if using
Dijon, you may need to
add a bit more sugar)

100 ml/⅓ cup rapeseed
or other neutral oil

salt and freshly ground
black pepper

piping/pastry bag

MAKES 2

Start by making the dill and mustard dressing.
Whisk the mustard, dill, vinegar and sugar in a
bowl with a good pinch of salt and pepper. Add
the oil carefully as you whisk: start by adding
a few drops, then begin steadily adding a thin
stream of oil. It should emulsify the dressing as
you continue to whisk. If you add it too quickly
it may split. Keep whisking until you have a
good, creamy consistency. Add a little bit more
oil if it is too thick.

Butter the bread and set aside.

Mix the potatoes with 2 tablespoons of the
dill and mustard dressing.

Top the bread evenly with the potato mix
to build height, then add the salmon on top.
Add some of the dill and mustard dressing,
then loosely roll the cucumber slices and place
2 pieces in the middle of each open sandwich.

Using the piping bag, pipe dollops of cream
cheese onto the sandwiches. Add the capers
and pickled tomato halves, and finish with a
grind of black pepper and dill sprigs to garnish.

LAKS MED AVOCADO
SMOKED SALMON & AVOCADO

This is a classic combination of smoked salmon and avocado. The tricky bit of using two soft toppings is that, unless you use a harder bread, the open sandwich risks feeling a bit mushy. To counteract this, add crunchy seeds and pickled onions. The pickled tomato adds balance to the softer flavours.

salted butter, for spreading

2 slices of rye bread, or 4 smaller slices (white bread also works, but do toast it or the overall sandwich might feel too mushy)

2 just-ripe avocados, halved and stoned/pitted

115 g/4 oz. smoked salmon

a squeeze of lemon juice

6–10 dollops of Herby Mayonnaise (see page 108)

6–8 pickled cherry tomato halves (see Cherry Tomato Quickle, page 114)

a few slices of Quick Pickled Red Onion (see page 115)

dill sprigs and Sticky Soya Seeds (see page 121), to garnish

piping/pastry bag

MAKES 2

Butter the bread and set aside.

Using a spoon, scoop out the avocado in whole pieces, taking care to keep it as intact as possible. Slice across in 3 mm/⅛ inch thick slices, then gently press down to allow the pieces to fan to one side slightly. Using a spatula, move the avocados to each slice of buttered bread and arrange 2 halves on each piece (or ½ avocado on each, if making 4 smaller open sandwiches).

Place the smoked salmon neatly on top of the avocado and squeeze a little lemon juice over. Using the piping bag, pipe a few dollops of herby mayonnaise on the sandwiches, then add the pickled tomatoes and onion. Garnish with sprigs of dill and a sprinkle of sticky soya seeds.

NORSK LAKS & EGG
SMOKED NORWEGIAN SALMON & EGG

Really good smoked salmon doesn't need very much messing with – and this version sells out as soon as it hits our café counter for breakfast, lunch and afternoons. We use a delicious Norwegian smoked salmon, but do use whichever kind you prefer.

salted butter, for spreading

2 slices of rye bread, or 4 smaller slices (softer white bread also works well)

3 hard-boiled/hard-cooked eggs

2 tablespoons mayonnaise

115 g/4 oz. smoked salmon

6–10 dollops of Herby Mayonnaise (see page 108)

a few slices of Quick Pickled Red Fennel (see page 115)

a few slices of Quick Pickled Red Onion (see page 115)

salt and freshly ground black pepper

pea shoots and dill sprigs, to garnish

piping/pastry bag

MAKES 2

Butter the bread and set aside.

Chop the boiled eggs and put in a bowl with the mayonnaise. Season with a bit of salt and some black pepper, then mix.

Spread the egg mayo on top of the buttered bread, ensuring you go right to the edges, but also creating height. Place the salmon neatly on top. Using the piping bag, pipe a few dollops of herby mayonnaise on each of the sandwiches, then add the pickled fennel and onion.

Garnish with pea shoots and dill sprigs, taking care to maintain the height of the open sandwich.

SENAPSSILL
MUSTARD HERRING

In Sweden, mustard herring is the king of the smörgåsbord. Often it is served as part of a buffet and not already on the bread, as it quickly soaks through. To avoid soggy bread, arrange and decorate the herring directly on a plate, then pass the bread around when serving.

salted butter, for spreading

2 slices of rye bread, or 4 smaller slices (white bread or Homemade Crispbread, see page 139, also work well)

a few lettuce leaves

2–4 cold cooked new potatoes

a few carrot crisps (see Vegetable Crisps, page 121)

pea shoots and dill sprigs, to garnish

MUSTARD HERRING

2 tablespoons Swedish mustard (Slotts Skånsk Senap is good) or a good, grainy sweet mustard

1 teaspoon Dijon mustard

1 tablespoon caster/superfine sugar

2 tablespoons white wine vinegar

2 tablespoons double/heavy cream

1 tablespoon crème fraîche or sour cream

1 small shallot, finely chopped

100 ml/⅓ cup neutral oil (such as sunflower)

2 tablespoons chopped dill

1 tablespoon chopped chives

150 g/5¼ oz. plain pickled Scandinavian herring (drained weight), cut into 2.5-cm/1-inch pieces

salt and freshly ground black pepper

MAKES 2

First make the mustard herring. In a bowl, mix together the mustards, sugar, vinegar, cream, crème fraîche and shallot, and season with salt and pepper. Slowly pour in the oil while whisking continuously, so that the sauce emulsifies and thickens. Add the dill, chives and herring. Cover and leave to marinate for a few hours in the fridge.

Butter the bread and top with salad leaves. Add the cold potatoes, then mustard herring on top. Top with crispy carrot slices and garnish with pea shoots and dill sprigs.

VEGGIE VERSION Replace the herring with Mushroom Quickle (see page 116).

SILDEMAD
ONION HERRING

This is the plain type of onion herring you will most often be served at restaurants. It doesn't need much other than dark, seeded rye bread and some onion and herbs on top. I do love to dress it up a little with some dollops of sour cream and leaves – and a glass of aquavit.

salted butter, for spreading

2 slices of dark rye bread, or 4 smaller slices

150 g/5¼ oz. pickled onion herring (drained weight)

2 tablespoons crème fraîche or sour cream

2 radishes, sliced

1 spring onion/scallion, sliced

dill sprigs, to garnish

piping/pastry bag

MAKES 2

Butter the bread and set aside.

Add the drained herring fillets to the rye bread so that they cover the base of the slice (wihout overlapping). It is important that the bread is well buttered as this will help to stop the herring juice from making the bread soggy.

Using the piping bag, pipe crème fraîche in several places across the sandwich. Add the sliced radishes and spring onion, then garnish with dill sprigs.

Enjoy immediately with a glass of aquavit (see page 12).

MARINERET SILD MED RØDBEDESALAT
PICKLED HERRING WITH BEETROOT

This is the most popular herring open sandwich we make at our café. It is not the most traditional, but a Swedish smörgåsbord often includes both pickled herrings and a beetroot salad – and the two go together well. This is a good herring option if you want to make the open sandwich a little bit ahead of time, as the beetroot mixture keeps the herring from soaking through to the bread. It works with most types of bread, but we always serve it on dark rye (as Danes do with all herring).

salted butter, for spreading

2 slices of dark rye bread, or 4 smaller slices

200 g/7 oz. Beetroot Salad (see page 118)

2 hard-boiled/hard-cooked eggs, halved

100 g/3½ oz. pickled onion herring (drained weight)

3 tablespoons chopped chives

freshly ground black pepper

micro herbs, to garnish

MAKES 2

Butter the bread and spread the beetroot salad on top. Add the halved eggs on top of the beetroot salad, then add the pickled herring (it's important to ensure it is well drained).

Top with the chopped chives, season with black pepper (salt won't be needed) and garnish with micro herbs.

KARRYSILD
CURRIED HERRING

Curried herring is probably the number one herring flavour in Denmark. It sounds peculiar to other nations that one should add pickled herring to a curried dressing, but somehow, this really does work well.

salted butter, for spreading

2 slices of rye bread,
   or 4 smaller slices

a handful of watercress
   or rocket/arugula

½ apple, thinly sliced

2 radishes, thinly sliced

1 boiled/cooked egg, cooked
   to the jammy stage, i.e.,
   slightly soft in the middle

micro herbs, to garnish

CURRIED HERRING

½ apple, peeled and finely
   chopped

1–2 gherkins, chopped

1 tablespoon capers,
   chopped

½ red onion, finely chopped

1 teaspoon mild curry
   powder

½ teaspoon turmeric
   (optional, for colour)

½ teaspoon Dijon mustard

100 ml/⅓ cup crème fraîche
   or sour cream

50 ml/3½ tablespoons
   mayonnaise

150 g/5¼ oz. plain pickled
   Scandinavian herring
   (drained weight), cut into
   2.5-cm/1-inch pieces

salt and freshly ground
   black pepper

MAKES 2

First make the curried herring. Add the apple, gherkins, capers and onion to a bowl and stir in the curry powder, turmeric (if using), mustard, crème fraîche, mayonnaise, ½ teaspoon salt and some pepper. Add the herring, cover and transfer to the fridge for a few hours for the flavours to develop.

Butter the bread and arrange the watercress or rocket on top. Add the curried herring, followed by the sliced apple and radishes. Top each sandwich with half an egg, then garnish with micro herbs.

VEGGIE VERSION Replace the herring with Mushroom Quickle (see page 116).

REJER I TRÆNGSEL
DANISH-STYLE PRAWNS

In Denmark, if the prawns are served without egg, an open sandwich is served on white bread. The word trængsel *means 'squished', so literally translated, this would be 'squished prawns'. However, this looks stylish and pretty as a picture.*

salted butter, for spreading

2 slices of soft white bread

150 g/5¼ oz. cooked prawns/
   shrimp

40 ml/3 tablespoons mayonnaise

salt and freshly ground black
   pepper

dill sprigs and edible flowers,
   to garnish

grated lemon zest and a squeeze
   of juice, to serve

piping/pastry bag

MAKES 2

Butter the bread. Arrange the prawns in rows on the bread, then use the piping bag to pipe mayonnaise between the rows. Season with salt and pepper.

Add the dill sprigs and edible flowers on top to garnish, then finish with some grated lemon zest and a squeeze of lemon juice to serve.

VARIATION Instead of dill sprigs, you can garnish these open sandwiches with any micro herbs that work flavour-wise. Baby sorrel looks really pretty.

RÄKMACKA
SWEDISH-STYLE PRAWNS

Ask any Nordic person, mostly Swedes, about the traditional prawn/shrimp sandwich and they will most often associate it with boat trips to neighbouring countries. Big open sandwiches loaded with delicious fresh North Sea prawns, are a total abundance of the sea. These are a meal in themselves – so if you're lucky enough to have access to a lot of fresh prawns and you want a treat lunch, this is the one to make.

I'll bet that no matter how many prawns you add to this, most homesick Swedes would still feel the need to add more. This is the only time where Swedes do not adhere to a lagom *amount of something!* Lagom *means 'not too much, not too little – just right – always in balance and never over the top' as is the Swedish way.*

salted butter, for spreading

2 slices of Swedish flat bread or white bread of your choice

a few lettuce leaves

2 hard-boiled/hard-cooked eggs

50 ml/3½ tablespoons mayonnaise

150 g/5¼ oz. cooked prawns/ shrimp (the prawns are the star here)

a few strips of cucumber

1 baby radish, thinly sliced

salt and freshly ground black pepper

pea shoots, to garnish

lemon wedges, to serve

piping/pastry bag

MAKES 2

Butter the bread and place the lettuce leaves on top.

Slice the eggs using an egg slicer. Place an egg on each sandwich and fan out on one side of the bread.

Using a piping bag, pipe a generous dollop of mayonnaise in the middle, then pile the prawns on the sandwiches. Top with another dollop of mayonnaise and season with salt and pepper.

Top with the cucumber strips and sliced radish. Garnish with pea shoots, then serve with lemon wedges for squeezing over.

SKAGENRÖRA

TOAST SKAGEN

One of the most famous open sandwiches in Sweden, skagenröra is most often served on a fried or toasted piece of white bread. At the café we serve this in several ways. On weekends, we might use a soft white bread like franskbrød (see White Loaf with Poppy Seeds, page 136) or a toasted sourdough, or alternatively, we might opt for a rye flat bread. During the week, when a lot of our customers opt for healthier options, we serve it on seeded rye.

Some Swedes use this as a topping on hot dogs, which are almost as popular as open sandwiches in Scandinavia. First, they add a wiener sausage to a hot dog bun, then add condiments and a good dollop of skagenröra. Some also add mashed potatoes. We know how bad this sounds, but is actually delicious.

salted butter, for spreading

2 slices of white bread, or 4 smaller slices (toasted, if preferred)

a few curly endive leaves

salt and freshly ground black pepper

pea shoots, to garnish

grated lemon zest and a squeeze of juice, to serve

SKAGENRÖRA SALAD

50 ml/3½ tablespoons mayonnaise

100 ml/⅓ cup crème fraîche or sour cream

2 tablespoons finely chopped dill, plus extra sprigs to serve

2 tablespoons finely chopped chives

1 shallot, finely chopped

¼ teaspoon grated lemon zest

¼ teaspoon fresh grated horseradish (or from a jar, but check the strength)

¼ teaspoon Dijon mustard

a squeeze of lemon juice

salt and freshly ground black pepper

200 g/7 oz. good-quality cooked North Atlantic prawns/shrimp

MAKES 2

First make the *skagenöra* salad. Mix everything together (except the prawns) and adjust the seasoning to taste. Add the prawns and stir – then taste again. Leave for at least an hour to allow the flavours to mingle.

Butter the bread and place the leaves on top of the bread, followed by the *skagenröra*.

Season with salt and pepper and garnish with pea shoots. Finish with some grated lemon zest and a squeeze of lemon juice to serve.

VARIATIONS

Instead of just prawns, try a mixture of prawns and crayfish tails in the *skagenröra*.

If you have some leftover smoked salmon pieces, chop and add to the *skagenröra*.

If you need to make this go further without adding to the price, add a few finely chopped crab sticks to the *skagenröra*.

ÆG OG REJER
EGG & PRAWNS

At the café, this outsells everything. We use Scandinavian prawns/shrimp that are hand peeled – because they taste best.

People often ask when prawns should be served on rye and why they are most often served on white bread. Aside from simply being a personal preference, we feel that if the egg is the bigger part of the smørrebrød, then it works best on rye to contrast the softness of the egg. In the case of this smørrebrød, the egg dominates and therefore we chose rye bread. The herby mayo goes so well on this against the salty prawns. No wonder it's been a bestseller day-in and day-out for almost two decades at ScandiKitchen.

For any prawn sandwich you make, choose prawns that have bite and taste nice. We realize not everyone can get prawns fresh off the boat, but prawns in brine often retain good flavour – even frozen ones do, at times, taste better than some of the supermarket chilled varieties.

salted butter, for spreading

2 slices of rye bread, or 4 smaller slices (white bread can also work here, or Swedish flat bread)

4 hard-boiled/hard-cooked eggs

4–6 tablespoons Herby Mayonnaise (see page 108)

100 g/3½ oz. cooked small prawns/shrimp

a handful of cress

salt and freshly ground black pepper

micro herbs, to garnish

grated lemon zest and a squeeze of juice, to serve

piping/pastry bag

MAKES 2

Butter the bread and set aside.

Using an egg slicer, slice the boiled eggs and arrange them neatly across the bread (at our place, we sit two whole eggs onto one large open sandwich in two rows).

Use the piping bag to pipe a generous amount of herby mayonnaise down the middle. Arrange the prawns to one side of this, then, on the other side, add a generous amount of cress, all the way along (using the mayo to make it stick).

Season with salt and pepper, garnish with micro herbs, then finish with some grated lemon zest and a squeeze of lemon juice to serve.

FISKEFILLET MED REMOULADE
BREADED PLAICE WITH DANISH REMOULADE

You can use shop-bought breaded fish or coat your own (see instructions below).
If you can't get plaice, then flounder, sole, pollock or dab work well, too. This open
sandwich should be served warm, not hot.

salted butter, for spreading

2 slices of rye bread,
   or 4 smaller slices

2 cooked breaded fish fillets,
   traditionally plaice (shop-
   bought or see right)

2 tablespoons Remoulade
   (see page 117)

2 tablespoons capers

1 radish, thinly sliced
   (optional)

dill sprigs and micro herbs,
   to garnish

lemon wedges, to serve

MAKES 2

Butter the bread and arrange the cooked fish over it. Top each sandwich with a good dollop of remoulade, followed by the capers and radish slices (if using).

Garnish with dill sprigs and micro herbs, and serve with lemon wedges for squeezing.

VEGGIE VERSION Breaded parsnips work well instead of fish – and they taste great with the remoulade.

HOW TO BREAD FISH Lightly dust the fish fillets with plain/all-purpose flour, then dip in beaten egg, before coating in breadcrumbs. Heat a glug of neutral oil (such as sunflower) in a frying pan/skillet and fry the fish for 1–2 minutes on each side until done (this will depend on the thickness of the fish).

STJERNESKUD
BREADED PLAICE, ASPARAGUS & PRAWN

In traditional open sandwich restaurants, you will find a fish sandwich called 'shooting star'. It was invented at Davidsen, which was the open sandwich restaurant in Copenhagen. It was named after the Soviet cosmonaut Yuri Gagarin – with the fish, and asparagus, presented to stand like a rocket – very delightfully old-school.

salted butter, for spreading

2 slices of rye bread or toasted white bread

2 cooked breaded fish fillets, traditionally plaice (see opposite)

70 g/2½ oz. cooked prawns/ shrimp

4–6 spears asparagus, blanched

a squeeze of lemon juice

salt and freshly ground black pepper

dill sprigs, to garnish

DRESSING

2 tablespoons mayonnaise

2 tablespoons crème fraîche or sour cream

a few drops of Worcestershire sauce

1 teaspoon tomato purée/ paste

2 tablespoons ketchup

a squeeze of lemon juice

a pinch of paprika

MAKES 2

Mix all the ingredients for the dressing together in a bowl.

Butter the bread and arrange the cooked fish on top. Top with the dressing, then the prawns and asparagus. Add a squeeze of lemon juice, season with salt and pepper, and garnish with dill sprigs.

ÄGG OCH KAVIAR
EGG & AVOCADO WITH ROE SPREAD

This is probably the most famous breakfast sandwich in Sweden. Although this would not be described as a true open sandwich, it deserves a mention as it is delicious and so easy to make – and I see no reason why it can't be enjoyed all day long. In fact, at our café we serve it on our lunch menu from time to time (both with or without avocado, and most often using a plain boiled egg instead of poached). The roe is Kalles Kaviar, *a Swedish favourite, and hugely popular in our shop.*

salted butter, for spreading

2 slices of rye bread, or 4 smaller slices (you can use any bread you like – although if you use crispbread, it can be hard to eat this using a knife and fork)

2 just-ripe avocados, halved and stoned/pitted

2–4 tablespoons *Kalles Kaviar* (Swedish caviar spread)

1 tomato, sliced (optional)

4 boiled/cooked eggs, cooked to the jammy stage, i.e., slightly soft in the middle

salt and freshly ground black pepper

a few watercress or other leaves, to garnish

MAKES 2

Butter the bread and set aside.

Using a spoon, scoop out the flesh of the avocados. Using a fork, smash the avocado and season with salt and pepper. Spread the avocado onto the bread so you have a thick layer on each open sandwich. If you prefer, you can also slice the avocados for a prettier look.

Squeeze the *Kalles Kaviar* on top of the avocado, adding 1–2 tablespoons to each sandwich, to taste. Add a sliced tomato, if you like, then slice the eggs and arrange on top. Season with salt and pepper.

Garnish with a few watercress leaves and serve.

VEGGIE VERSION It is now possible to get a vegetarian version of *Kalles Kaviar* that tastes very similar to the original.

FISKEFRIKADELLER
FISH CAKES

This is the most traditional way to eat fish cakes in Denmark – on rye bread with a good dollop of remoulade. There are many types of fish cake. Swedish, Norwegian, Danish... I couldn't possibly find room for them all here, so we decided to add the recipe that we eat most often on a traditional Danish open sandwich. Feel free to mix these up with your own flavour combinations and different herbs: it's a versatile recipe. Fiskekaker (Norwegian fish cakes) are very similar to this recipe, but often include ground nutmeg.

salted butter, for spreading

2 slices of rye bread, or 4 smaller slices

a good handful of green leaves or pea shoots

2 tablespoons Remoulade (see page 117)

6–8 pickled cherry tomato halves (see Cherry Tomato Quickle, page 114)

a few slices of Quick Pickled Red Onion (see page 115)

4–6 capers (optional)

dill sprigs, to garnish

FISH CAKES

250 g/9 oz. cod (or haddock, pollock or other white fish)

1 teaspoon flaked salt

50 ml/3½ tablespoons double/ heavy cream

1 egg

2–3 tablespoons plain/all-purpose flour (note this can really vary depending on the fish)

1 tablespoon cornflour/cornstarch

salt and freshly ground black pepper

large knob/pat of butter and a dash of neutral oil (such as sunflower oil), for frying

MAKES 2

First, make the fish cakes. In a food processor, add the fish and salt and pulse well until blended (it is important to salt and process the fish first). Add the cream, egg and flour (start with 2 tablespoons flour, but you might need to add a bit more later on) and process until well combined. Add the cornflour, combine and season. Transfer the mixture to the fridge for 1 hour before using.

Heat a large frying pan/skillet and add a good knob of butter and a glug of oil. Using a tablespoon and the palm of your (wet) hand, shape the mixture into 6 egg-sized balls. Add them to the frying pan and squash them down gently nto loose patties to give them a slightly flatter surface.

Fry until golden brown and crisp on both sides, 2–3 minutes per side. You may want to try one first and assess if its firm enough to stay together – if not, add a bit more flour. You don't want them to fall apart in the pan, but adding too much flour isn't nice.

Butter the bread and arrange the green leaves on the bread. Place the fish cakes on top (you may need to slice them slightly, depending on sizing).

Add a generous dollop of remoulade, then add the pickled tomatoes, pickled red onion and capers, if using. Garnish with dill sprigs.

GUBBRÖRA
EGG & ANSJOVIS

Gubbröra *means 'old man's mix' in Swedish. Yes, it's not a great name when literally translated – but I guess it's meant in a 'stuff granddads eat on their open sandwich' sort of way. It's a very traditional open sandwich topping, most often eaten with crispbread (but equally delicious on other breads).*

In Scandinavia, ansjovis *confusingly doesn't mean anchovies, but instead means pickled sprats. They come in a little tin, usually from the brand ABBA (nothing to do with the group) and are the same brined fish used for Jansson's temptation potato dish. If you can't get hold of them, you can use an equivalent weight of plain pickled herring instead –* matjes *(young) herrings also work.*

salted butter, for spreading

2 pieces of crispbread
(see Homemade Crispbread,
page 139)

a few salad leaves

1–2 radishes, thinly sliced

sprigs of dill and chopped chives,
to garnish

GUBBRÖRA

125 g/4 oz. Swedish pickled sprat
fillets (such as Abba's *Grebbestad
ansjovis*)

1 small red onion

4 hard-boiled/hard-cooked eggs

1 tablespoon capers

2 tablespoons chopped chives

2 tablespoons chopped dill

3–4 tablespoons crème fraîche
or sour cream

1 teaspoon *Kalles Kaviar*
(Swedish caviar spread, optional)

salt and freshly ground black
pepper

MAKES 2

First make the *gubbröra*. Drain the sprats, set 4 aside and roughly chop the rest. Cut a few rings of red onion and set them aside, then finely chop the rest. Finely chop the eggs and mix together with the chopped sprats, onion and eggs.

Add the capers, chives, dill, crème fraîche, *Kalles Kaviar*, salt and pepper, and mix it all together to form a creamy mixture.

Butter the crispbread, the add some salad leaves. Spread the *gubbröra* mixture on top of the salad leaves, then add the sliced radish and reserved red onion rings. Roll up the reserved sprats and arrange two on each open sandwich.

Garnish with sprigs of dill and chopped chives.

RØGET MAKREL MED ÆRTER
SMOKED MACKEREL WITH PEAS

A fresh summer open sandwich that has stood the test of time as a special guest on our menu at the cafe. If you are not a mackerel fan, this works well with other hot-smoked fish too, such as trout or salmon.

salted butter, for spreading

2 slices of dark rye bread, or 4 smaller slices

¼ small fennel bulb

¼ green apple

a squeeze of lemon juice

a drizzle of olive oil

100 g/¾ cup frozen peas

2 tablespoons chopped chives

1 tablespoon chopped tarragon

115 g/4 oz. smoked mackerel fillets, skins removed

salt and freshly ground black pepper

dill sprigs, to garnish

MACKEREL DRESSING

2 tablespoons honey

1 tablespoon red wine vinegar

1 teaspoon wholegrain mustard

MAKES 2

Combine the dressing ingredients and set aside.

Butter the bread and set aside.

Finely shave the fennel with a mandoline (or with a super-sharp knife) and place in a bowl. Then shave the apple in the same way. Combine the apple and fennel, then dress with few drops of lemon juice and olive oil. Season with salt and pepper.

Cook the peas in salted boiling water for 1 minute, then refresh in cold water to stop the cooking. Crush the peas with a fork, add the chives and tarragon, a few drops of lemon juice and olive oil, and season. Spread the crushed peas on the bread.

Place a generous piece of mackerel on the pea mixture and brush with the dressing.

Top with the fennel mixture, season and garnish with dill sprigs.

RØGET MAKREL MED ÆG
SMOKED MACKEREL WITH SCRAMBLED EGG

Mackerel is the fish from my corner of Denmark. As kids, we used to go with our parents to the local harbour and buy it freshly smoked – there really are few scents that bring me back home to a warm summer's day in Reersø better than the smell of freshly smoked fish and sea air.

salted butter, for spreading

2 slices of rye bread, or 4 smaller slices

2 eggs

a knob/pat of butter

a few salad leaves

140 g/5 oz. smoked mackerel fillets

1 portion of Mackerel Dressing (see opposite, optional)

salt and freshly ground black pepper

chopped chives and pea shoots, to garnish

MAKES 2

Butter the bread and set aside.

Whisk the eggs together. Heat a bit of butter in a small pan, then add the eggs and gently scramble until just cooked. Take off the heat immediately and season.

Arrange the leaves and mackerel on the buttered bread and brush with the dressing, if using. Top with the still-warm eggs, then season and garnish with chives and pea shoots.

VARMRÖKT LAX
HOT-SMOKED SALMON

It can be tricky to make flaked fish look pretty on an open sandwich – it doesn't look particularly attractive just placed on top of a slice of bread. At the café, we make a really lovely dressing and carefully fold the hot-smoked fish flakes into it, then use that to top the bread. Never mix it too much – just gently fold through. This open sandwich is a summer bestseller for us. It is light, fresh and tangy, and reminds us of midsummer days back home. It also goes well in a white baguette or you can serve the hot-smoked salmon mixture with a simple salad.

salted butter, for spreading

2 slices of rye bread, or 4 smaller slices

2 curly endive leaves or other green leaves

6–8 pickled cherry tomato halves (see Cherry Tomato Quickle, page 114)

a few slices of Quick Pickled Red Onion (see page 115)

1 radish, thinly sliced

salt and freshly ground black pepper

pea shoots, to garnish

HOT-SMOKED SALMON MIXTURE

50 ml/3½ tablespoons crème fraîche or sour cream

¼ cucumber, deseeded and chopped into 5-mm/¼-inch cubes

½ apple, chopped into 5-mm/¼-inch cubes

4 radishes, finely chopped

a bunch of dill, finely chopped

1 small shallot, finely chopped

a squeeze of lime juice

115 g/4 oz. hot smoked salmon, gently flaked

salt and freshly ground black pepper

MAKES 2

For the hot-smoked salmon mixture, mix all the ingredients together, except for the salmon. You want a creamy, rough mix that shows the pieces and all the colours of the vegetables and herbs. Season well, then gently fold through the salmon.

Butter the bread and arrange the curly endive leaves on top. Spoon the hot-smoked salmon mix on top.

Place the pickled tomato halves and pickled red onion on top of the mix and finish with the thinly sliced radish. Season, then garnish with pea shoots.

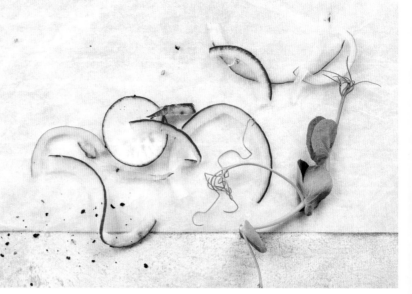

MEAT & POULTRY

FRIKADELLER
DANISH MEATBALLS

Cold Danish meatballs are delicious however they are served. At the café we have started adding a finely chopped potato salad to ours – it really adds to the texture and is also a nod to the classic Danish summer dish of meatballs and potato salad – all on one slice.

This really is a full lunch in itself if you go for a whole slice of rye bread – if you're serving alongside other things, reduce or remove the potato salad or serve on smaller pieces of bread.

salted butter, for spreading

2 slices of rye bread, or 4 smaller slices

1 portion of Potato Salad (see page 118)

4–6 Danish Meatballs (see page 126), cold or slightly warmed

pickled beetroot/beets (use shop-bought or see Pickled Beetroot, page 111), drained well, to taste

pickled cucumber (use shop-bought or see Cucumber & Dill Quick Pickle, page 114), to taste

a few slices of Quick Pickled Red Onion (see page 115) or raw red onion

chopped chives and parsley leaves, to garnish

MAKES 2

Butter the bread, then add a small layer of potato salad to cover the bread.

Slice the meatballs to fit the base of the bread – if they are on the smaller side, it is easier to split them in half rather than slice.

Top with the beetroot, cucumber and onion and garnish with finely chopped chives and thyme sprigs.

KÖTTBULLAR
SWEDISH MEATBALLS

Across every café and deli in Sweden, you will find a version of a köttbullemacka
– a meatball open sandwich. This is Comfort Food 101, and the one all Swedes have
grown up eating. Store-bought meatballs work well, as does store-bought beetroot
salad. Making your own is next level though.

We're aware this sandwich has looked the same since forever. Some things we
just don't change and we're not about to start.

salted butter, for spreading

2 slices crusty bread, such as franskbrød (see White Loaf with Poppy Seed, page 136) or flat bread

115 g/4 oz. Beetroot Salad (see page 118, enough to generously fit the base of the bread slices)

10 Swedish Meatballs (see page 127), or use fewer and slice them if they are large

pickled cucumber (use shop-bought or see Cucumber & Dill Quick Pickle, page 114), to taste

6 pickled cherry tomato halves (see Cherry Tomato Quickle, page 114)

salt and freshly ground black pepper

micro herbs, to garnish

MAKES 2

Butter the bread and spread the beetroot salad on the bread. Arrange the meatballs on top.

Add the pickled cucumber and tomatoes, season and garnish with micro herbs.

ROASTBEEF MED BEARNAISE DRESSING
ROAST BEEF WITH BEARNAISE

While this is not traditional, there is just something utterly delicious about bearnaise sauce. I often make this at home with leftover roast beef. If I have store-bought bearnaise, I use this – otherwise I simply make my tarragon mayonnaise.

salted butter, for spreading

2 slices of dark rye bread, or 4 smaller slices (or toasted sourdough or white bread, such as franskbrød (see White Loaf with Poppy Seed, page 136)

a few baked potato slices (see Vegetable Crisps, page 121, but cut into thick slices and baked longer, or use thick-cut salted potato chips)

170 g/6 oz. rare roast beef (we use thick-cut steak, cooked rare, then cooled and sliced, any leftover roast beef also works)

4 generous tablespoons bearnaise sauce or Tarragon Mayonnaise (see page 109)

50 g/1¾ oz. Quick Pickled Red Onion (see page 115)

4 sun-dried tomato or pickled cherry tomato halves (see Cherry Tomato Quickle, page 114)

salt and freshly ground black pepper

thyme sprigs, to garnish

piping/pastry bag

MAKES 2

Butter the bread. Arrange the potato slices on the bread, followed by the cold beef slices.

Use the piping bag to pipe dollops of the bearnaise sauce across the top.

Add the pickled onion and tomatoes, then season with salt and pepper. Garnish with thyme sprigs.

ROASTBEEF
ROAST BEEF ON RYE

One day when Jonas and I happened to be in the small Danish town of Vejle, we visited a tiny little café called Onkel A. There, we had the tallest open sandwiches we've ever had. If you ever happen to pass by Vejle, we recommend you pay this place a visit. Under their roast beef, the chef added a light potato and carrot salad, an idea we borrowed for our special at the café. Is it traditional? Nope. Is it good? Yep. This adds flavour and height.

salted butter, for spreading

2 slices of dark rye bread, or 4 smaller slices

170 g/6 oz. rare roast beef (we use thick-cut steak, cooked rare, then cooled and sliced, any leftover roast beef also works)

2 tablespoons Horseradish Cream (see page 86)

4 tablespoons Remoulade (see page 117)

a few slices of Quick Pickled Red Onion (see page 115)

pickled cucumber (use shop-bought or see Cucumber & Dill Quick Pickle, page 114), to taste

a few Crispy Onions (see page 120)

salt and freshly ground black pepper

micro herbs, to garnish

CARROT & POTATO SALAD

100 g/3½ oz. carrots, peeled

100 g/3½ oz. potatoes, peeled

20 g/¼ cup grated mature/sharp cheese

20 g/1½ tablespoons salted butter

salt and freshly ground black pepper

MAKES 2

Start by making the carrot and potato salad. Cut the carrots and potatoes into 1-cm/½-inch chunks, then boil them until just cooked. Drain and immediately mix with the grated cheese and butter. Season and leave to cool down slightly.

Butter the bread and arrange the carrot and potato mixture on top. Arrange the slices of beef on top.

Add the horseradish cream, remoulade, pickled onion, pickled cucumber and a few rings of crispy onion. Season with salt and pepper, and garnish with micro herbs.

SOMMER KYLLING
SUMMER CHICKEN

When asparagus is in season, this one is just the ticket. The basil
works so well with both the creamy chicken and the asparagus.

salted butter, for spreading

2 slices of dark rye bread,
   or 4 smaller slices

6–8 spears asparagus

4 tablespoons mayonnaise

½–1 teaspoon Dijon mustard,
   to taste

2 tablespoons chopped chives

3 tablespoons chopped basil

200 g/7 oz. cooked chicken,
   chopped (leftovers from the
   Sunday roast work great)

1 just-ripe avocado, halved
   and stoned/pitted

a few salad leaves

a few thin slices of cucumber

1–2 radishes, thinly sliced

salt and freshly ground black
   pepper

micro herbs, to garnish

MAKES 2

Butter the bread and set aside.

Blanch the asparagus in boiling water for 2 minutes,
then plunge into cold water to stop the cooking process.

Mix the mayonnaise, mustard, chives and basil together,
then season with salt and pepper.

Set aside 2 whole asparagus spears, then cut the rest into
bite-sized pieces and add to the dressing. Add the chicken
and stir. Check the seasoning again.

Using a spoon, scoop out the avocado in whole pieces and
slice each half thinly. Add half a sliced avocado to each piece
of buttered bread, then add the salad leaves and top with
the chicken mixture.

Arrange the cucumber and radish slices on top, then garnish
with micro herbs

TIP The chicken mixture also works really well as a filling
for closed sandwiches.

KARRYKYLLING
CURRIED CHICKEN

At times, we make specials at the café that are just so lovely we keep them around for longer. This is one of those open sandwiches – not traditional, but it is so popular in our café it would be wrong not to include it in this book. I'm not sure if the popularity is because it's a tribute to the curried coronation chicken so beloved in Britain (we made this when Queen Elizabeth had her jubilee), or just because the flavours work so well. Either way, we're keeping it around.

salted butter, for spreading

2 slices of rye bread, or 4 smaller slices

a few mini poppadoms (optional, but these add a nice crunch)

8 pickled cherry tomato halves (see Cherry Tomato Quickle, page 114)

a few slices of Quick Pickled Red Onion (see page 115) or raw red onion

2 tablespoons Crispy Onions (see page 120) or crispy bacon pieces

salt and freshly ground black pepper

pea shoots and apple slices, to garnish

CURRIED CHICKEN

½ apple, finely chopped

a squeeze of lemon juice

150 g/5¼ oz. cooked chicken breast, chopped into bite-sized pieces

50 g/3½ tablespoons mayonnaise

1 heaped tablespoon mango chutney

2 heaped tablespoons Greek yogurt

1 stick/rib celery, finely chopped

1 spring onion/scallion, chopped

1 teaspoon white wine vinegar

½ teaspoon medium curry powder

salt and freshly ground black pepper

MAKES 2

For the curried chicken, drizzle the apples with a squeeze of lemon juice, then add all the rest of the ingredients and stir together. Taste and adjust the seasoning.

Butter the bread and top each buttered bread slice with the chicken mixture. Place a few mini poppadoms on the chicken and top with the pickled tomatoes and red onion.

Finish with crispy onions, then season and garnish with pea shoots and apple slices.

HØNSESALAT
CHICKEN & BACON

You will find a variation of this open sandwich all over Denmark, sometimes with asparagus, sometimes not – sometimes with mushrooms, sometimes only bacon. If you prefer it plainer, make this one yours by adding or removing things as you prefer. I absolutely love crispy chicken skin on top as it gives great crunch and flavour. If you're serving straight away, try toasting the rye bread and serving the open sandwich slightly warm.

salted butter, for spreading

2 slices of dark rye bread, or 4 smaller slices (or toasted sourdough or white bread)

4–5 rashers of streaky/fatty bacon

a few salad leaves

6 pickled cherry tomato halves (see Cherry Tomato Quickle, page 114)

micro herbs and Crispy Chicken Skin (see page 120), to garnish

CHICKEN MIXTURE

100 g/3½ oz. mushrooms, sliced

100 g/3½ oz. asparagus, blanched, or 1 jar white asparagus, drained (100 g/ 3½ oz. drained weight)

200 g/7 oz. cooked chicken, chopped (leftovers from the Sunday roast work great)

50 g/3½ tablespoons crème fraîche or sour cream

50 g/3½ tablespoons mayonnaise

1 teaspoon Dijon mustard

1 teaspoon dried tarragon

a squeeze of lemon juice

2 tablespoons chopped chives

salt and freshly ground black pepper

MAKES 2

Butter the bread and set aside.

Fry the bacon until crisp and set aside to drain on kitchen paper and allow to cool.

To make the chicken mixture, fry the mushrooms in the pan you used for the bacon until cooked (the bacon fat gives great flavour). Transfer to a bowl.

Roughly chop the asparagus and add to the mushrooms with the cooked chicken and all the remaining chicken mixture ingredients. Mix together and leave for a few minutes for the flavours to mingle. Taste and season.

To assemble, add some salad leaves to the buttered bread, then top with a generous amount of the chicken mixture. Arrange the bacon and tomatoes on top, and garnish with micro herbs and crispy chicken skin.

HAMBURGERRYG MED ITALIENSK SALAT

PORK LOIN WITH ITALIAN SALAD

What the Danes call 'Italian salad' is, perhaps oddly, called a 'Russian salad' in Italy (insalata russa – although it is made with potato rather than asparagus). Incidentally, a 'Russian salad' in Denmark is beetroot/beets. Perhaps some Danes went on holiday and returned with a fancy new recipe and it just became known as something from Italy.

Nevertheless, this mayo-based topping is most often served with smoked ham. It is also very delicious with chicken, so if you're not feeling very traditional, there is room to experiment here.

salted butter, for spreading

2 slices of rye bread, or 4 smaller slices (also tastes great on white bread)

a few salad leaves

8 slices of Danish-style smoked pork loin (*hamburgerryg*), Polish sopocka or a nice smoked ham

6–8 pickled cherry tomato halves (see Cherry Tomato Quickle, page 114)

salt and freshly ground black pepper

micro herbs and crispy carrots (see Vegetable Crisps, page 121), to garnish

ITALIAN SALAD

75 g/⅔ cup cubed carrots

75 g/⅔ cup frozen peas

4–6 spears asparagus

50 g/3½ tablespoons crème fraîche or sour cream

50 g/3½ tablespoons mayonnaise

a squeeze of lemon juice

salt and freshly ground black pepper

MAKES 2

First, make the Italian salad. Cook the carrots in boiling water until al dente, then drain and set aside.

Blanch the peas and asparagus, then drain. Chop the asparagus, reserving a few of the tips for the garnish.

Mix all ingredients for the Italian salad together.

Butter the bread and add some salad leaves to the base of the rye bread to give it a bit of height. Arrange the smoked ham on top, then add a generous amount of the Italian salad.

Add the cherry tomatoes, season and garnish with micro herbs and crispy carrots.

TIP Out of asparagus season, use frozen asparagus or white asparagus from a jar.

FLÆSKESTEG
ROAST PORK

If you have leftover pork from a roast, this is a delicious and very traditional open sandwich – one you will find at most deli counters all year round in Denmark. I will say that this one will always have an old-school look. On the flip side, if it ain't broke...

Like I say, you don't need to make a big roast to make this – use leftovers if you have them, or even store-bought. A fattier pork works, too, such as belly. Crackling is great on this if you have it, but you can use pork scratchings instead, if you can get hold of them – I have done this in the past and just crunch them up a bit to use as a garnish.

salted butter, for spreading

2 slices of rye bread, or 4 smaller slices

200 g/7 oz. roast pork, sliced (keep the crispy crackling on, if it has it)

2 generous tablespoons Red Cabbage (see page 110), well drained

pickled cucumber (use shop-bought or see Cucumber & Dill Quick Pickle, page 114), to taste

a few slices of Quick Pickled Red Onion (see page 115)

1–2 tomatoes, deseeded and chopped

a few slices of Quick Pickled Red Onion (see page 115) or raw red onion

thyme sprigs, to garnish

MAKES 2

Butter the bread and then arrange the slices of pork across the bread. In Denmark, the slices are reasonably thick, around 5 mm/¼ inch. It needs to be a substantial amount of pork.

Add the red cabbage, followed by the cucumber, red onion and tomatoes. Season and garnish with some thyme sprigs.

TIP If you're using leftover pork that feels a little dry (as can easily happen the day after), add a bit of spiced mayo under the pork – try the Mustard Mayonnaise (see page 109) or mix grainy mustard with natural yogurt for a less oily dressing.

VARIATION Another famous way of serving this is as a *flæskestegssandwich* (roast pork sandwich). The toppings are the same, but serve the meat slightly warmed, in a crusty white bun instead of on rye bread, with lots of red cabbage. This works especially well with fattier cuts of meat and is absolutely delicious.

BØF TARTAR
STEAK TARTARE

This is a delicious open sandwich, which should be served on rye bread in my opinion. Some toast the bread, but I prefer it as is.

salted butter, for spreading

2 slices of dark rye bread, or 4 smaller slices

225 g/8 oz. beef fillet, chilled (see note)

1 teaspoon mustard (Dijon or English)

1 shallot, finely chopped

1 tablespoon chopped parsley

a drizzle of olive oil

a few drops of Worcestershire sauce (optional)

2 egg yolks

a few red onion rings

2 tablespoons capers

a few crispy parsnips or carrots (see Vegetable Crisps, page 121)

salt and freshly ground black pepper

micro greens, to garnish

MAKES 2

NOTE ON EATING RAW BEEF
Safety is paramount when eating raw beef. Only use a good cut from a butcher (beef fillet really is the best cut for tartare) and use it on the day you buy it. Pop the meat in the freezer for a bit before chopping to firm it up so it's easier to handle, then serve it immediately after preparing.

Butter the bread and set aside.

Take the super-cold meat out of the freezer (see note) and, using a very sharp knife, chop into very fine and small pieces. While using a knife is the traditional way, you can, like me, use a food processor (just pulse it a few times).

Mix with the mustard, shallot, parsley, a dash of good olive oil, salt and pepper. You can also add a few drops of Worcestershire sauce, to taste.

Arrange the meat on the buttered bread and make a small well in the middle to fit an egg yolk. Carefully add an egg yolk to each sandwich, then add the raw onion rings, capers and crispy parsnips or carrots. Garnish with micro greens.

PARISERBØF
BEEF WITH FRIED EGG

In Denmark, you find this served both as an open sandwich and as a main, with bread on the side. Essentially, it's a burger patty with an egg on top, either raw, poached or fried. I prefer fried, but any will work – and all are very nice. In Denmark, the name is pariserbøf, *which translates as 'Parisian steak'. It is most often served on lightly toasted white bread, but rye bread also works.*

salted butter, for spreading
and cooking
2 slices of white bread, toasted
250 g/9 oz. minced/ground beef
1 tablespoon Dijon mustard
a knob/pat of unsalted butter
a drizzle of oil
2 eggs
2 tablespoons Horseradish Cream
(see page 86)
2 tablespoons capers
a few red onion rings
a few Vegetable Crisps
(see page 121)
salt and freshly ground
black pepper
pea shoots, to garnish

MAKES 2

Butter the toasted bread and set aside.

Combine the beef with the mustard, salt and pepper, and shape into 2 patties. In a pan, add a bit of butter and a glug of oil, and fry the patties until medium (still a bit red in the middle).

In a frying pan/skillet, fry the eggs until still runny in the middle. Alternatively, you can use the egg yolks raw.

Add the beef patty to the buttered toast, then add the egg (if using raw, discard the whites and serve the yolk in the shell or a small bowl on the side).

Decorate with dollops of horseradish cream, capers, onion rings and vegetable crisps. Finish off with pea shoots to garnish.

TIP Don't overcook the beef patty, it needs to be juicy.

LEVERPOSTEJ MED BACON
LIVER PÂTÉ WITH BACON

Liver pâté is the go-to open sandwich topping for most Danes. From fancy open sandwiches to school lunches, we eat a lot of it. Getting the right liver pâté outside of Denmark is hard – and while you can make your own, it is laborious and doesn't quite taste the same, even if you put in the effort. I suggest finding a local pâté that you like (a smooth-style paté works well, rather than a coarser Ardennes-type).

salted butter, for spreading

2 slices of rye bread, or 4 smaller slices

5–7 mushrooms, sliced

4–6 rashers of streaky/fatty bacon

neutral oil (such as sunflower oil), for frying

140 g/5 oz. pork liver pâté, or whatever pâté you prefer

pickled beetroot/beets (use shop-bought or see Pickled Beetroot, page 111), drained well, to taste

8 pickled cherry tomato halves (see Cherry Tomato Quickle, page 114)

micro herbs and thyme sprigs, to garnish

MAKES 2

Butter the bread and set aside.

Fry the mushrooms and bacon in a little oil until cooked and the bacon is crispy, then allow to drain on a paper towel.

Either slice the pâté and place it on the bread or spread it if that is easier. You need quite a thick layer (at least 5 mm/ ¼ inch). Arrange the beetroot, bacon and mushrooms on top of the pâté, then the tomato halves, finishing off with micro herbs and a thyme sprigs to garnish.

VARIATIONS In Denmark, pâté is often served with a lean salt beef. It is not quite the same as the salt beef you can buy elsewhere – it is a different cut from the cow and is salted slightly differently and sliced thinly. However, it's a workable substitution to use the salt beef available to you as long as you have thin slices. Use buttered rye bread, a layer of pâté, then a layer of thinly sliced salt beef, topped with raw red onion rings and cress (and some jellied aspic, if you like). This version is called *dyrlægens natmad*, or the 'veterinarian's night snack' – reputedly named after a regular at the iconic Davidsen smørrebrød restaurant in Copenhagen.

SPEKESKINKE MED FERSKEN
AIR-CURED HAM WITH PEACHES

In Norway, spekeskinke – similar to air-cured ham – is often served on open sandwiches, especially around 17th May, which is Norway's national day. I love pairing it with classics such as peaches or pears and bitter leaves. Any air-dried ham (such as Parma ham) is fine, so whatever you can get hold of will work.

I love whipping the Brie and spreading it on – it goes nice and fluffy. However, if you can't be bothered, just add it in nice slices.

1 x 200-g/7-oz. piece of Brie, chilled

salted butter, for spreading

2 slices of crusty white bread, toasted if you like

1 peach, stoned/pitted and cut into 8 slices

6–8 walnuts halves, lightly crushed

1 teaspoon honey

a few rocket/arugula leaves

6 slices air-dried ham

salt and freshly ground black pepper

pea shoots, to garnish

MAKES 2

First, cut the rind off the Brie – it must be chilled when you do this, or it is impossible. Cut the Brie into pieces and then leave to come to room temperature. Whip it for 4–5 minutes with a whisk until it is nice and fluffy.

Butter the bread and set aside.

Griddle the peach slices on a ridged griddle/grill pan, then set aside.

Toast the walnuts in the same hot pan until lightly toasted, then turn off the heat and add a dash of honey – just enough to coat. Season lightly.

Spread the whipped cheese on the buttered bread, then add some rocket leaves. Arrange the ham and peaches across the bread, then add the toasted honey walnuts. Season and garnish with pea shoots.

VEGGIE

ASPARGES OG POCHERET ÆG
ASPARAGUS & POACHED EGG

This is a lovely open sandwich to make when asparagus is in season. I love the taste of freshly blanched asparagus, almost al-dente, and the softness of the avocado and poached egg on top – spring on an open sandwich. Make sure you add some crunch on top as this one has a lot of soft elements. If you don't have crispy seeds, you can use toasted sesame seeds or even some crispy onions.

butter, for spreading

**2 slices of rye bread, or 4 smaller
slices**

**15–20 asparagus tips (enough
to cover both slices of bread)**

2 eggs

vinegar, for poaching

**3–4 tablespoons Herby Mayonnaise
(see page 108)**

**1 just-ripe avocado, halved,
stoned/pitted and sliced**

**salt and freshly ground black
pepper**

**micro herbs and Sticky Soya Seeds
(see page 121), to garnish**

**store-bought Hollandaise dressing,
to serve (optional)**

MAKES 2

Butter the bread and set aside.

Blanch the asparagus tips in boiling water, then chill them in cold water to stop the cooking. Set aside.

Prepare the poached eggs by bringing a pan of water to a simmer. Add a dash of vinegar. Create a vortex with a spoon and drop in the first egg to cook. Cook to medium softness, then drain on a paper towel. Repeat with the second egg. It's fine if the eggs cool down a bit – this is not a hot sandwich.

Smear some of the herby mayo on the buttered bread. Place the asparagus on the bread all along the base so it is covered, with all the spears facing the same direction. If the asparagus spears are thick, you might need to cut them lengthways down the middle, then place flat-side down.

Arrange half the sliced avocado on each slice of bread. Add some more herby mayo, and top each sandwich with a poached egg.

Season, then garnish with micro herbs and sticky seeds. Serve with Hollandaise drizzled on top, if you like.

ÆG OG RØDBEDESALAT

EGG & BEETROOT

This is just such a nice combination – boiled egg paired with a simple beetroot/ beet salad. This is one of those open sandwiches you are unlikely to find on a menu in Scandinavia, but at the café in London, this has grown in popularity over the years. There is something about the sharp taste of beetroot in this creamy dressing that just goes so well with boiled egg. The soya seeds on top add a bit of crunch – but you could also add some chopped toasted nuts if you prefer.

butter, for spreading

2 slices of dark rye bread, or 4 smaller slices (white bread or Homemade Crispbread, see page 139, also work well)

200 g/7 oz. Beetroot Salad (see page 118)

3–4 hard-boiled/hard-cooked eggs, quartered

3 tablespoons chopped chives

micro herbs and Sticky Soya Seeds (see page 121, optional), to garnish

MAKES 2

Butter the bread and spread the beetroot salad on top, all the way to the edges.

Arrange the quartered eggs on top and then the chives. Garnish with micro herbs and sticky soya seeds, if you like.

ÆGGESALAT
CURRIED EGG MAYO

This is a staple on the Danish lunch table. It is interesting how Scandinavians use curry powder the way we do, considering these spices are not generally found in our traditional recipes.

Essentially, this is egg mayo. In Sweden, they would not use the curry powder but might add a bit of pickle. It's a delicious base for an open sandwich, and I often add a few pieces of crispy bacon or pancetta on top too.

butter, for spreading

2 slices of dark rye bread, or 4 smaller slices

a few salad leaves

2–4 long thin slices of cucumber

1–2 radishes, thinly sliced

2 rashers of streaky/fatty bacon (optional)

pea shoots and Sticky Soya Seeds (see page 121), to garnish

EGG MIXTURE

5 just-hard-boiled/just-hard-cooked eggs

130 g/generous ½ cup mayonnaise

2 tablespoons crème fraîche or sour cream

½ apple, finely chopped

1 teaspoon medium curry powder

¼ teaspoon turmeric (optional; this will make it bright yellow)

50 g/½ cup pickled cucumber (use shop-bought or see Cucumber & Dill Quick Pickle, page 114)

½ teaspoon Dijon mustard

2 tablespoons chopped chives

1 tablespoon capers, chopped

salt and freshly ground black pepper

MAKES 2

First make the egg mixture. Roughly chop the eggs and mix with the other ingredients. Cover and set aside for at least 30 minutes for the flavours to develop.

Butter the rye bread. Add the leaves, then top with the egg mixture.

Loosely roll the cucumber slices on top to create some height. Add the radish slices and the bacon (if using), then garnish with pea shoots and sticky soya seeds.

TIP This egg mixture also goes well with pickled herring, bacon, ham and salmon.

MISO BLOMKÅL OG ESTRAGON
MISO CAULIFLOWER & TARRAGON

The traditional smørrebrød repertoire is not vegetarian-friendly. In Scandinavia, vegetarianism and veganism didn't really become prevalent until recently – and for years, vegetarians were served cheese on rye as standard. Thankfully, this has now changed.

At the café, we have several veggie and vegan open sandwiches permanently on the menu, along with many special guests. This particular one is always a huge favourite with our customers.

butter, for spreading

2 slices of rye bread, or 4 smaller slices

4 tablespoons Tarragon Mayonnaise (see page 109)

6 pickled cherry tomato halves (see Cherry Tomato Quickle, page 114)

25 g/3 tablespoons toasted hazelnuts, crushed slightly

salt and freshly ground black pepper

micro herbs, to garnish

MISO CAULIFLOWER

1 tablespoon miso paste

1 tablespoon oil

250–300 g/9–10 oz. cauliflower (if there are any inner leaves, keep these – they taste great)

salt and freshly ground black pepper

MAKES 2

Start by making the miso cauliflower. Preheat the oven to 170°C (325°F) Gas 3.

Mix the miso and oil together with 2 tablespoons water and season. Cut the cauliflower into small florets and mix with the miso seasoning. Place on an oven tray and roast until done – about 15 minutes, depending on the size of your florets (you want the cauliflower to still have some crunch).

Butter the bread, then spread the tarragon mayonnaise on it. Place the cauliflower florets on the bread to cover the mayo, then add the tomatoes and toasted hazelnuts. Season with salt and pepper, and garnish with micro herbs.

KARTOFFELMAD
NEW POTATO

Danes love cold new potatoes on open sandwiches. When we first served this at the café, we struggled to persuade people that cold potatoes taste great in and on sandwiches. We do understand the reluctance – however, when in season, new potatoes are so delicious on rye bread, and this is now a firm favourite.

butter, for spreading

2 slices of rye bread, or 4 smaller slices

2 tablespoons Herby Mayonnaise (see page 108)

4–5 cold, cooked new potatoes (more, if on the smaller side)

2 tablespoons mayonnaise

6–8 pickled cherry tomato halves (see Cherry Tomato Quickle, page 114)

a few slices of Quick Pickled Red Onion (see page 115) or raw red onion

1–2 radishes, thinly sliced

a few Crispy Onions (see page 120)

micro herbs and Sticky Soya Seeds (see page 121), to garnish

piping/pastry bag (optional)

MAKES 2

Butter the bread, then spread it with a layer of herby mayo.

Slice the cold potatoes and arrange neatly on top.

Top with any remaining herby mayo and the plain mayonnaise across the potatoes (easier to use a piping bag), then add the tomatoes and onion, radish and crispy onions.

Season well with salt and pepper, and garnish with micro herbs and sticky soya seeds.

VARIATIONS

Use garlic mayonnaise (see Garlic Mayonnaise, page 108, or use store-bought) instead of plain mayonnaise for a bit of a kick.

For a meaty addition, you can add crispy bacon pieces, too.

BUTTERNUT MED FETA OST OG GRØNKÅL
BUTTERNUT SQUASH WITH FETA & KALE

Another café favourite, the roasted butternut squash not only gives a pop of colour, but is delicious. I love crispy kale and add our sticky soya seeds for a bit of umami flavour and crunch.

250–300 g/9–10½ oz. peeled butternut squash, cut into 7.5 mm/½ inch thick slices
½ teaspoon paprika
olive oil, for brushing
100 g/3½ oz feta cheese
1 tablespoon cream cheese or crème fraîche
butter, for spreading
2 slices of rye bread, or 4 smaller slices

a few slices of red onion
salt and freshly ground black pepper
micro herbs and Sticky Soya Seeds (see page 121), to garnish

CRISPY KALE CHIPS
3–4 large kale leaves
1 tablespoon olive oil

piping/pastry bag

MAKES 2

Preheat the oven to 170°C (325°F) Gas 3.

Brush the butternut squash slices with a little oil, then season with salt and pepper and the paprika. Roast in the oven for 20–30 minutes until just cooked, depending on how thick the slices are.

Meanwhile, for the crispy kale chips, remove the tough stems from the leaves and place them on a baking tray with a small glug of oil. Roast in the oven for about 10 minutes until crispy. Set aside to cool and crisp up.

Mash the feta with a fork and add the cream cheese or crème fraîche to bind it together. Spoon into a piping bag.

Butter the bread and arrange the roasted butternut squash on the bread. Pipe several generous dollops of the creamed feta across the top. Add the crispy kale and red onion slices. Season well and garnish with micro herbs and sticky soya seeds.

MAKE IT VEGAN Use a vegan cream cheese and feta, and make the sticky soya seeds with maple syrup instead of honey.

DILLMARINERET GULEROD MED AVOCADO
DILL-MARINATED CARROT WITH AVOCADO

There will be some marinated carrots leftover, which will be delicious enjoyed in a salad. Do note that you will probably need to marinate the carrots overnight so factor in enough time to allow for this preparation.

butter, for spreading

2 slices of rye bread, or 4 smaller slices (both white or rye bread works well here)

1 avocado, halved, stoned/pitted and sliced

dill sprigs and Sticky Soya Seeds (see page 121), to garnish

a few Crispy Kale Chips (see opposite), to serve (optional)

MARINATED CARROTS

4 carrots

2 tablespoons olive oil

2 tablespoons apple cider vinegar

1 teaspoon liquid smoke, such as hickory (can be found online)

3 tablespoons chopped dill

1 teaspoon soft brown sugar

a few black peppercorns

½ teaspoon mustard seeds

salt and freshly ground black pepper

a pinch of paprika

a sheet of dried nori or a pinch of dried seaweed flakes (optional)

MAKES 2

Start with the marinated carrots. Cook the carrots whole in boiling water until al dente (no more or they will be mushy and impossible to slice). Add to cold water to stop the cooking process and cool.

Using a peeler or mandoline, shave long strips of carrot lengthways, trying to keep each slice intact.

Put the rest of the marinated carrot ingredients in a ziplock bag, then add the carrot slices. Squeeze to remove the air, then seal and place in the fridge to marinate for at least 12 hours, but ideally 24 hours.

Butter the bread and arrange the sliced avocado on top. Roll up the carrot slices and add to give the sandwich height. Season, then garnish with dill and sticky soya seeds. Serve with crispy kale, if using.

SVAMPE
MUSHROOM

I'm aware that this is 'just' mushrooms on toast. However, I'm including this because in Scandinavia, autumn/fall is a time when many people go into the forest to pick chanterelles to take home, clean, fry over a high heat and enjoy on warm, buttered bread.

Seeing as we don't all have access to forests and chanterelles (or the knowledge to identify them safely), I make this at home when I find fine-looking wild mushrooms at the shops. Or just nice mushrooms of any kind.

Ricotta goes well on this, adding a delicious creaminess, but you can stay traditional and leave it out if you prefer.

400 g/14 oz. chanterelles or mixed fresh mushrooms of your choice, sliced

salted butter, for cooking and spreading

a few thyme sprigs

2 large slices of white sourdough bread, or 4 smaller slices

100 g/scant ½ cup ricotta

salt and freshly ground black pepper

MAKES 2

Heat a frying pan/skillet but do not add any oil – it needs to be dry. Add the sliced mushrooms to the hot pan. Cook, stirring occasionally, and wait for the water to start coming out of the mushrooms – be patient. The mushrooms will go wet and then their water will evaporate. Once this starts to happen, add a good knob of butter, some salt and pepper and a sprig of thyme. The mushrooms are done.

Toast the bread, butter it and add a generous layer of ricotta on top. Top with the mushrooms and garnish with the rest of the thyme sprigs.

RÖDBETSTARTAR
BEETROOT TARTARE

This takes a little effort to make, but as far as a veggie open sandwich goes, this is both beautiful and delicious. Sometimes I make the tartare at home as a starter to a meal and serve toasted rye bread on the side. Any leftover tartare can be used in salads the day after. I prefer this with a poached egg, but some use raw egg yolk. If you want to make this vegan, simply leave out the egg (and make the horseradish cream with a dairy-free mayo).

butter, for spreading

2 slices of rye bread, or 4 smaller slices

3 tablespoons hazelnuts

2–4 eggs

vinegar, for poaching

1 just-ripe avocado, halved, stoned/pitted and thinly sliced

2 tablespoons Horseradish Cream (see page 86)

1 teaspoon chopped dill, plus sprigs to garnish

a few crispy parsnips (see Vegetable Crisps, page 121)

a few Crispy Onions (see page 120)

pea shoots, to garnish

BEETROOT MIXTURE

100 g/3½ oz. cooked beetroot/beets

50 g/1¾ oz. pickled beetroot/beets (use shop-bought or see Pickled Beetroot, page 111), drained

1 tablespoon capers

1 small shallot, finely chopped

¼ apple, finely chopped

2–3 cornichons, finely chopped

1 teaspoon Dijon mustard

1 teaspoon chopped dill

a few drops of Worcestershire sauce

1 tablespoon chopped flat-leaf parsley

a dash of extra virgin olive oil

6.5-cm/2½-inch round cookie cutter

MAKES 2

To make the beetroot mixture, grate the cooked and pickled beetroot and place in a bowl. Add the other ingredients and stir to combine with a dash of olive oil (the mustard and oil help to bring the mixture together a bit so it does not fall apart).

Butter the bread and set aside. Toast the hazelnuts in a frying pan/skillet and leave to cool, then roughly chop.

Prepare the poached eggs by bringing a pan of water to a simmer. Add a dash of vinegar. Create a vortex with a spoon and drop in the first egg to cook. Cook to medium softness, then drain on a paper towel. Repeat with the second egg. It's fine if the eggs cool down a bit – this is not a hot sandwich.

Arrange half the sliced avocado on each slice of bread. Carefully place the cookie cutter on one of the sandwiches and fill with half of the beetroot mixture. Press gently to shape (if making smaller ones, this does not work as easily, so you are better off arranging with a spoon). Carefully pull the cookie cutter away and the beetroot mixture should stay in shape. Repeat on the other sandwich.

Top the sandwiches with the poached eggs (alternatively, use the raw egg yolk: separate the yolk from the egg white, add the yolk to half the eggshell and place this on top of the beetroot).

Add dollops of horseradish cream, then the toasted hazelnuts, chopped dill, crispy parsnips and crispy onions. Garnish with pea shoots and dill sprigs.

TIPS If serving with raw egg yolk, add a few onions rings as this complements it well.

Using pre-cooked beetroot/beet is fine, but if you cook your own, boil until tender, then peel and leave to cool.

SOMMERSALAT
SUMMER SALAD

Sommersalat is a topping that is quite traditional, but hard to make outside Denmark, as the traditional smoked cheese we call rygeost is almost impossible to export due to its very short shelf life. Living overseas, I've always used cottage cheese instead – it's healthy, great tasting and good value.

This salad is often served on its own on rye bread, but I recommend you serve it with avocado as shown here – it gives a wonderful visual contrast against the white and red of the radishes. If you eat fish, then hot-smoked salmon or smoked mackerel also work well.

butter, for spreading

2 slices of rye bread, or 4 smaller slices

a handful of rocket/arugula

1 avocado, halved, stoned/pitted and sliced (or 100 g/3½ oz. hot-smoked salmon or smoked mackerel, flaked)

1 radish, thinly sliced

micro herbs and dill sprigs, to garnish

HORSERADISH CREAM

30-g/1-oz. piece of horseradish, peeled and grated

200 ml/1 scant cup crème fraîche or sour cream

lemon juice, to taste

a small squeeze of honey

salt and freshly ground black pepper

SUMMER SALAD MIXTURE

200 g/1 scant cup cottage cheese

6–8 radishes, sliced

2 spring onions/scallions, sliced

¼ cucumber, deseeded and chopped

2 tablespoons chopped chives

a squeeze of lemon juice

1 small teaspoon Horseradish Cream (see left)

a drizzle of honey

salt and freshly ground black pepper

MAKES 2

To make the horseradish cream, mix the ingredients together and adjust the seasoning to taste. If you prefer a milder taste, simply add less horseradish. Set aside.

Combine the summer salad ingredients, season to taste and set aside.

Butter the bread and arrange the rocket on the bread. Add the sliced avocado (or flaked fish) and top with the summer salad and sliced radish. Season and garnish with micro herbs or dill.

TIP You need only a small amount of the horseradish cream for the summer salad, but it keeps for several days in the fridge. It does develop a stronger taste after a day or two though, so be careful if you don't like too much heat.

BLÅ OST MED FIGEN OG HONNING
BLUE CHEESE WITH FIGS & HONEY

*Cheese on open sandwiches can sometimes look a bit boring, so I do like
to jazz things up with some textures and garnish. One of the most popular
combinations in Sweden at Christmas is to eat blue cheese on ginger biscuits
(it is delicious) – so I've added some broken ginger biscuits as crunch here.*

butter, for spreading

2 slices of rye bread,
  or 4 smaller slices

30 g/generous ¼ cup
  walnut halves

1 teaspoon honey

100 g/3½ oz. blue cheese of
  your choice (creamy Danish
  Blue works well here)

a few salad leaves (a sweeter
  leaf works against the
  blue cheese)

½ pear, thinly sliced

1 fig, quartered

1–3 Swedish-style ginger
  thin biscuits, to taste

micro herbs, to garnish.

MAKES 2

Butter the bread and set aside.

Lightly crush the walnuts, then toast them in a
frying pan/skillet. Turn off the heat and add the
honey. Stir to coat the nuts, then leave to cool.

Neatly slice the blue cheese and arrange on the
bread. Arrange the leaves on top, along with the
thinly sliced pear and fig quarters.

Add the honey nuts, then break the ginger thins
and arrange them on top for a rustic look. Garnish
with a few micro herbs.

OST MED RØDLØG
STINKY CHEESE WITH RED ONION

*A meal of open sandwiches often ends with cheese – either on a cheese board
or on more open sandwiches. Danbo is a cheese beloved by many Danes. It has
a particularly pungent smell to it, but the taste is delicious. In our house, it's
known as 'the stinky cheese'. Such strong cheeses need sweet and sour to balance
them, so the red onion relish works well here. If you cannot get hold of Danbo,
Riberhus is another Danish alternative – otherwise, a strong semi-soft cheese
of your choice will do.*

butter, for spreading

2 slices of rye bread, caraway
bread or sourdough bread,
or 4 smaller slices

30 g/generous ¼ cup walnut
halves

70 g/2½ oz. Danbo, or a
mature/sharp semi-soft
cheese, neatly sliced

2–4 tablespoons Red Onion
Relish (see page 117, or use
store-bought), to taste

2 radishes, thinly sliced

1 spring onion/scallion, sliced

micro greens, to garnish

MAKES 2

Butter the bread and set aside.

Lightly crush the walnuts, then toast them
in a frying pan/skillet. Set aside to cool.

Arrange the cheese on the bread.
Add the relish and top with
the sliced radishes, spring
onion and toasted
walnuts. Garnish
with micro greens.

SVAMPE MED MISO
MUSHROOMS WITH MISO

The bean base for this makes a larger portion than needed for these two sandwiches but keeps for several days in the fridge. It's delicious as a side to other things, too. This is one of the most popular veggie open sandwiches in our café.

2 slices of crusty bread

6 pickled cherry tomato halves (see Cherry Tomato Quickle, page 114)

micro herbs, to garnish

a few Crispy Kale Chips (see page 80), to serve (optional)

CANNELLINI SPREAD

1 x 400-g/14-oz. can cannellini beans, drained (drained weight about 240 g/9 oz.)

2 garlic cloves, crushed

100 ml/⅓ cup extra virgin olive oil

100 g/3½ oz. sun-dried tomatoes

salt and freshly ground black pepper

juice of ½ lemon, or to taste

MISO MUSHROOMS

250 g/9 oz. chestnut mushrooms

1 tablespoon miso paste

salt and freshly ground black pepper

MAKES 2

For the cannellini spread, combine all the ingredients, blend in a food processor until smooth and season. Set aside.

For the miso mushrooms, cook the mushrooms in a saucepan (I prefer to dry fry until the mushrooms release their water and then it evaporates, but if you don't want to wait, you can add a little oil). When cooked through, stir through the miso paste and season.

Spoon 2–3 tablespoons of the cannellini bean paste on each piece of bread. Add the miso mushrooms and pickled tomatoes. Garnish with micro herbs and serve with crispy kale chips.

TIP The rest of the cannellini bean spread will keep in the fridge for up to 3 days – use it as a spread or dip.

TOMAT OG ÆG ELLER KARTOFFEL
TOMATO & EGG OR POTATO

This may seem a simple topping for an open sandwich, but when in season, the humble tomato proves a great host on an open sandwich. We eat these several ways, mainly simply sliced on rye bread with sea salt and maybe some chives. Here, I'm taking things further with two versions – one with boiled egg and the other with new potato. As I've said earlier in this book, potato on an open sandwich seems to divide people, but Danes absolutely love it.

butter, for spreading

2 large slices of rye bread

2 hard-boiled/hard-cooked eggs, or 2–4 new potatoes, boiled, cooled and sliced

2 large ripe tomatoes (1 per open sandwich)

1–2 tablespoons mayonnaise or garlic mayonnaise (store-bought or see Garlic Mayonnaise, page 108; this is especially nice on the potato option), to taste

2 tablespoons very finely chopped chives

micro herbs, Crispy Onions (see page 120) and Sticky Soya Seeds (see page 121), to garnish

DRESSING

1–2 tablespoons extra virgin olive oil

1 teaspoon balsamic vinegar

½ shallot, finely diced

a pinch of sugar

1 teaspoon finely chopped parsley

1 teaspoon finely chopped tarragon (use dried if you don't have fresh)

pinch of ground coriander

salt and freshly ground black pepper

piping/pastry bag

MAKES 2

Combine all the dressing ingredients and set aside. Butter the bread.

For the tomato and egg, arrange the sliced egg on the base of the bread, followed by the sliced tomato. Drizzle the dressing on the tomato. Use the piping bag to pipe mayonnaise on the sandwiches, then add the chopped chives. Garnish with micro herbs of your choice, crispy onions and sticky soya seeds

For the tomato and potato, arrange the potato slices on the base of the bread, followed by the sliced tomato. Drizzle the dressing on top, then use the piping bag to pipe garlic mayonnaise on top and add the chopped chives. Garnish with micro herbs of your choice, crispy onions and sticky soya seeds.

RØDBEDEHUMMUS MED AVOCADO
BEETROOT HUMMUS WITH AVOCADO

This vegan open sandwich is really popular in the café. As we have very little tradition to draw from when we create vegan options, we enjoy playing with different flavours. Our love of beetroot really shines in a hummus – especially when served on a delicious piece of rye bread with fresh avocado.

vegan spread, for spreading

2 slices of rye bread,
   or 4 smaller slices

100 g/3½ oz. Quick Beetroot
   Hummus (see below)

1 just-ripe avocado, halved
   and stoned/pitted

4 long thin slices of cucumber

3–4 radishes, sliced

salt and freshly ground
   black pepper

micro herbs and Sticky Soya Seeds
   (see page 121), to garnish

QUICK BEETROOT HUMMUS

1 x 400-g/14-oz. can chickpeas/
   garbanzo beans, drained
   (240 g/9 oz. drained weight)

50 ml/3½ tablespoons olive oil

100 g/3½ oz. pickled beetroot/
   beets (use shop-bought or see
   Pickled Beetroot, page 111),
   drained (reserve some of the
   liquid)

1 garlic clove, crushed

1 tablespoon tahini

juice of ½ lemon, or to taste

1 teaspoon ground cumin

salt and freshly ground black
   pepper

MAKES 2

To make the beetroot hummus, rinse the chickpeas, then blend with the oil. Add the pickled beetroot and blend until incorporated. Add the other ingredients and a bit of the beetroot brine, then season well. If it feels too dry, add a bit of cold water and blend again. This will keep in the fridge for up to 3 days.

Spread the vegan spread on the bread. Spread 100 g/3½ oz. of the beetroot hummus on top and spread over the sandwich lightly with a spoon so no corners are showing.

Using a spoon, scoop out the avocado in whole pieces, taking care to keep it as intact as possible. Slice across in 3-mm/⅛-inch thick slices, then gently press down to allow the pieces to fan to one side slightly. Using a spatula, transfer the avocado halves carefully onto the hummus.

Loosely roll the cucumber slices and arrange on top. Add the radish slices, then season and garnish with micro herbs and sticky soya seeds.

PARTY
FOOD

NINE CANAPÉS

Open sandwiches can make superb canapés, but simply cutting them into smaller pieces won't work. You can absolutely use the same recipes as for the larger open sandwiches, but with consideration for how the toppings and dressings look on a smaller piece of bread (as well as how many toppings a canapé base can hold). Guests should be able to hold a drink in one hand and a canapé in the other – and they should be able to eat it in a single mouthful. For pre-dinner drinks, plan 3–4 per person; for an event with no dinner to follow, plan 5–7 per person. The more drinks you serve at your event and the longer it goes on, the more canapés people will eat. These recipes all make 10 canapés.

EGG & BEETROOT

3 hard-boiled/hard-cooked eggs
10 x 3-cm/1¼-inch squares
   of buttered rye bread
4 tablespoons Beetroot Salad
   (see page 118)
a few toasted hazelnuts,
   lightly crushed
micro herbs, to garnish

Slice the egg (you need an egg slicer for the slices to be neat – it's very hard to do with a knife). Use the larger slices on the bread, one per square (you will have some left over, as only the larger slices will fit).

Pulse the beetroot salad slightly in a food processor, or chop a bit more by hand – only enough so that it is possible to spoon it out over the egg without it looking messy. Spoon it on the egg.

Add a few toasted hazelnut pieces and garnish with micro herbs.

ROAST BEEF

10 x 3-cm/1¼-inch circles
   of buttered rye bread
150 g/5¼ oz. Remoulade (see page
   117, blended slightly for piping)
200 g/7 oz. rare roast beef,
   very thinly sliced
3 tablespoons Horseradish Cream
   (see page 86)
20 shallot rings
1–2 cornichons, sliced
salt and freshly ground black pepper
micro herbs, to garnish

2 piping/pastry bags

Use the piping bag to pipe remoulade on each circle of bread – this will help to secure the beef in place. Arrange 20 g/¾ oz. beef on each circle of bread – arrange it with a bit of height.

Pipe each canapé with a touch of horseradish cream, then top each one with 2 raw shallot rings and a cornichon slice. Season and garnish with micro herbs.

MINI FISH CAKES

10 mini fish cakes, cooked (see Fish
   Cakes, page 37, but make 10 mini
   fish cakes with the mixture)
10 x 3-cm/1¼-inch squares
   of buttered rye bread
4 tablespoons Remoulade
   (see page 117)
10 small capers
3–4 radishes, sliced
10 small pieces of Quick Picked
   Red Onion (see page 115)
micro herbs, to garnish.

piping/pastry bag

Add the fish cakes to the buttered bread, then add remoulade to the piping bag and pipe 3 dollops on top of each fish cake.

Add the capers, radish slices and one little piece of onion to each fish cake. Top with micro herbs.

These are best served a little warm, so try not to assemble them too far ahead of your event.

PICKLED HERRING

3 tablespoons cream cheese

1 tablespoon crème fraîche or sour cream

10 small pieces of well-drained pickled onion herring fillets that fit the sizes of the bread

10 x 3-cm/1¼-inch squares of buttered bread or rye crackers

3–4 long thin radishes, thinly sliced

salt and freshly ground black pepper

micro herbs, to garnish

piping/pastry bag

This one is a little tricky because herring soaks bread quickly, so you need to prepare these just before your guests arrive. Alternatively, decorate the herring pieces and transfer these to the bread just before serving.

Mix the cream cheese and crème fraîche together and season with salt and pepper to taste. Spoon into the piping bag.

Arrange the herring fillets on the bread, then pipe the creamy mixture in dollops across the fish. Arrange the sliced radish on top and garnish with micro herbs.

SKAGENRÖRA

10 x 3-cm/1¼-inch squares of toasted and buttered rye, sourdough or white bread

½ portion of Skagenrôra (see page 28, pulsed in the food processor to break down the prawns just a little)

20–30 cooked peeled prawns/shrimp

dill sprigs, to garnish

Top each buttered bread square with about 1 tablespoon of the skagenrôra, then arrange about 2–3 prawns on top of each canapé.

Season and garnish with dill sprigs.

TIP If your skagenrôra is a little watery, you can add some cream cheese to keep it together.

SALMON WITH AVOCADO CREAM

1 ripe avocado, halved and stoned/pitted

1 small teaspoon wasabi

2 generous tablespoons full-fat cream cheese

a squeeze of lemon juice, plus extra to serve

10 mini blini

140–200 g/5–7 oz. smoked salmon (depending on the blini size)

salt and freshly ground black pepper

dill sprigs, to garnish

grated lemon zest, to serve

piping/pastry bag

Scoop out the avocado flesh and mix with the wasabi, cream cheese and a few drops of lemon juice until smooth. Season well. Spoon into the piping bag.

Pipe a blob of the avocado onto each blini, then arrange the salmon on top – make sure to give it some height. Pipe more avocado cream on top and garnish with dill sprigs.

Season and top with a few drops of lemon juice and some zest to serve.

LIVER PÂTÉ

3 thin rashers of streaky/fatty bacon
100 g/3½ oz. smooth liver pate
10 x 3-cm/1¼-inch circles
    of buttered rye bread
3–4 cornichons, finely sliced
30 red currants
chopped chives and micro herbs,
    to garnish

If you can't get hold of *leverpostej*, choose any nice pâté. This can be quite a brown canapé, so make sure you use something colourful to finish it off.

Fry the bacon until very crisp, then leave to drain on a paper towel.

Either slice or spread the pâté on to the bread.

Cut the bacon into pieces and add one piece, standing on its side, to each canapé. Add the cornichon slices and red currants.

Top with chopped chives and sprigs of micro herbs to garnish.

BLUE CHEESE

50 g/generous ⅓ cup hazelnuts
1–2 teaspoons honey
110 g/½ cup creamy blue cheese
10 x 3-cm/1¼-inch squares
    of buttered dark rye bread
1–2 figs, sliced (depending on size)
3–4 tablespoons Red Onion Relish
    (see page 117 or use store-
    bought)
chopped chives and micro herbs,
    to garnish

Roughly chop the nuts and then toast in a hot frying pan/skillet. Take off the heat and immediately add the honey and stir to coat the nuts. Leave to cool.

Spread the cheese on the bread, then add a small piece of fig and top with the nuts and a small bit of onion relish.

Top with chopped chives and sprigs of micro herbs to garnish.

NEW POTATO & BACON

3 thin rashers of streaky/fatty bacon
3–4 new potatoes, cooked and
    cooled
10 x 3-cm/1¼-inch squares or
    rectangles of buttered rye bread
3–4 tablespoons mayonnaise
    or garlic mayonnaise
50 g/2½ oz. Quick Pickled Red
    Onion (see page 115)
salt and freshly ground black pepper
chopped chives and micro herbs,
    to garnish

piping/pastry bag

This is a great canapé for the summer. If you want to make it veggie, just leave out the bacon. You can instead add thinly sliced cherry tomatoes between the potato and mayo.

Fry the bacon until very crisp, then leave to drain on a paper towel.

Thinly slice the potatoes and add to the buttered bread. Pipe the mayonnaise on top in a pattern.

Cut the bacon into pieces and arrange on top. Add a few pickled red onion slices and season.

Top with chopped chives and sprigs of micro herbs to garnish.

LANDGÅNG
ALL-IN-ONE OPEN SANDWICH

This is another type of open sandwich not often seen outside our borders. Essentially, it is all-in-one piece of bread where you start at one end and go through various toppings. In Denmark, this often has everything from pâté to salami and cheese. In Sweden, a finer, decorated version is served at family gatherings, where you want a beautiful lunch with variety, but don't want to serve lots of open sandwiches. I stick to fish and egg because they go together. This is all about the presentation, making it beautiful and opulent without making it look over the top.

The bread is usually one long rectangular piece of white sandwich bread, about 7.5 x 12.5 cm/3 x 5 inches. In Sweden you can buy bread in this shape, but you could cut two pieces together and lay them side by side very closely (but be careful if you need to move them after making, if you do it that way).

butter, for spreading

2 rectangular slices of buttered soft white sandwich bread (about 12.5 x 7.5 cm/5 x 3 inches)

2 hard-boiled/hard-cooked eggs, sliced

4–5 tablespoons Hot-smoked Salmon (see page 42, or you can also simply use flaked hot-smoked salmon mixed with crème fraîche and lemon juice)

100 g/3½ oz. smoked salmon

1 avocado, stoned/pitted and sliced

50 g/1¾ oz. cooked peeled prawns/shrimp

6–8 thin slices of cucumber sliced lengthways (use a peeler or cheese slicer)

1 tablespoon mayonnaise

salt and freshly ground black pepper

peas, sliced radishes, dill sprigs and pea shoots, to garnish

a squeeze of lemon juice, to serve

piping/pastry bag

MAKES 2

Butter the bread and place it on the plates you wish to serve and eat from, to avoid any dramas moving it around.

Starting at one end, arrange boiled egg slices, then hot-smoked salmon mixture. In the middle, arrange the cold smoked salmon, followed by sliced avocado. Prawns follows this, then finally the cucumber ribbons.

Using a piping bag, dollop small amounts of mayonnaise across so there is an even amount (this is also to make sure the finishing garnishes stick).

Garnish with peas, sliced radishes for colour, dill sprigs and pea shoots. Drizzle the fish with a bit of lemon juice and season before serving.

TOPPINGS

ALL THE MAYONNAISES

Make your own mayo – or simply flavour a store-bought one as needed. At the café we use anything from herby and garlic to tarragon and mustard on our sandwiches – it's a quick way of adding extra flavour.

BASIC MAYONNAISE

2 egg yolks
1 teaspoon English mustard
250 ml/1 cup neutral oil,
    such as sunflower
½ teaspoon salt
freshly ground black pepper
a squeeze of lemon juice
a few drops of white wine
    vinegar (optional)

If using a blender, it is a bit easier make a batch with at least 2 yolks to make sure the blades get enough to work with. You can, of course, also whisk by hand.

Whisk the egg yolks and mustard until creamy, then slowly – very slowly – start adding the oil, whisking continuously. This is the most important bit to get it all to hang together – too fast, and it will split.

Keep going until you have the right consistency (add a little more oil if needed). Season with salt, pepper and a squeeze of lemon. If it's too thick, add a few drops of vinegar.

Store chilled. Eat within 2 days (as it contains raw egg).

GARLIC MAYONNAISE

You can either add 1–2 cloves of grated garlic to the Basic Mayonnaise (see left, adding at the same time as the mustard), or, if you're using store-bought, you can make a garlic mayonnaise by adding a grated clove of garlic to 100 ml/7 tablespoons mayonnaise (a little goes a long way here). You may want to season further with a bit of lemon juice – and for a fancier version, finely chopped parsley.

GOES WELL WITH *Prawn, beef, tomato, new potato.*

LEMON MAYONNAISE

Simply add lemon juice to taste to the Basic Mayonnaise (see left).

GOES WELL WITH *Anything fishy, most fresh veggie recipes.*

HERBY MAYONNAISE

230 ml/1 cup mayonnaise
    (see Basic Mayonnaise, left,
    or use store-bought)
3 tablespoons chopped dill
a handful of spinach
grated zest of ¼ lemon

Follow the Basic Mayonnaise recipe (see left) and blend in the dill, spinach and lemon zest at the end.

You can vary the herbs – add chives for a bit more punch, or chervil for a more aniseed note.

GOES WELL WITH (IF MADE WITH DILL) *Prawn, salmon, avocado, new potato, fried fish.*

TARRAGON MAYONNAISE

100 ml/7 tablespoons mayonnaise
(see Basic Mayonnaise, opposite
or use store-bought)
2 tablespoons tarragon leaves

Follow the Basic Mayonnaise
recipe (see opposite) and blend
in the tarragon at the end.

GOES WELL WITH *Beef, pork,
some chicken, cauliflower.*

MUSTARD MAYO

100 ml/7 tablespoons mayonnaise
(see Basic Mayonnaise, opposite
or use store-bought)
1–2 tablespoons grainy mustard,
to taste

Follow the Basic Mayonnaise
recipe (see opposite) and blend
in the mustard at the end.

GOES WELL WITH *Beef, pork, egg,
chicken, potato.*

WASABI MAYONNAISE

100 ml/7 tablespoons mayonnaise
(see Basic Mayonnaise, opposite
or use store-bought)
1 teaspoon wasabi paste

Follow the Basic Mayonnaise
recipe (see opposite) and blend
in the wasabi paste at the end.
You may want to add an extra
squeeze of lemon juice.

GOES WELL WITH *Salmon, prawn,
tuna, beef.*

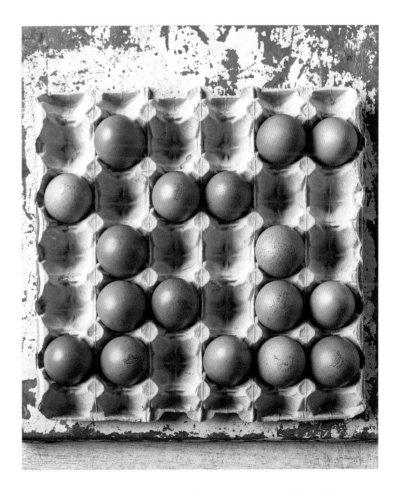

PICKLES, QUICKLES, A RELISH & A SAUCE

RØDKÅL
RED CABBAGE

The smell of red cabbage cooking instantly makes me feel at home and, if I close my eyes, I can almost be back in my childhood Christmas Eves (the main day in Scandinavia).

Red cabbage is a staple in all the Nordic countries at Christmas and the days that follow. During the rest of the year, we use it as a side, on open sandwiches and with meatballs. Red cabbage needs to be cooked longer than most other varieties, so I usually make this the day before, to save time and to allow the flavours to develop.

If you store this in sterilized jars it will keep for a long time (or about a week in the fridge, if you don't). The recipe used at Christmas is usually the same for every other time of the year, so it's very versatile.

50 g/3½ tablespoons unsalted butter

1 small red cabbage (about 500 g/ 1 lb. 2 oz.), thinly sliced, then chopped slightly

1 apple, peeled, cored and cut into small pieces

50 g/¼ cup light soft brown sugar

100 ml/⅓ cup blackcurrant cordial (redcurrant jelly can also be used)

50 ml/3½ tablespoons white wine vinegar

spices, to taste (star anise, bay leaf and allspice are all good options; my usual preference is a stick of cinnamon and a very small bit of clove)

salt and freshly ground black pepper

2 x 500-ml/16-fl oz. Kilner/Mason jars, sterilized

MAKES 1 LITRE/QUART

Melt the butter in a saucepan and add the cabbage. Allow to cook for a few minutes, then add the remaining ingredients and 100 ml/⅓ cup water, and bring to the boil. Turn down the heat and simmer on low, covered, for about 2 hours. Check it from time to time to see if it needs topping up with water.

Once the cooking time is up, check the seasoning, then leave to simmer, uncovered, for a further 30 minutes (again, check the water levels regularly). You need a good balance of not too sour and not too sweet so keep tasting to assess the salt, vinegar and sugar levels. My mother always said, 'It should not irritate any areas of your tongue when you taste it!'

Remove and discard any hard spices before serving.

TIP If you prefer a crunchier red cabbage, you can reduce the cooking time by more than half – for open sandwiches in the summer, a crunchier cabbage often gives a fresher result.

GOES WELL WITH *Pork, meatballs, veggie balls, pâté, ham. Also used as a side dish for warm meals.*

SYLTEDE RØDBEDER
PICKLED BEETROOT

Scandinavian pickled veg tends to be sweeter than other European pickles.
This recipe is sweet, but not overly so, and has a good bite and sharpness.
Use these as decoration or to make Beetroot Salad (see page 118).
I love a bit of horseradish, so I usually add this when making at home.
If you don't love a kick, just leave it out – or vary your spices to suit.
Most spices you add will give a subtle flavour, not a strong one.

800 g/1 lb. 12 oz. fresh beetroot/
   beets
1 teaspoon coarse salt
1 cinnamon stick
10 peppercorns
1 tablespoon mustard seeds
4 bay leaves
400 ml/1¾ cups white wine
   vinegar (6% acidity)
200 g/1 cup caster/superfine sugar
1 small slice of fresh horseradish
   (optional)

2 x 500-ml/16-fl oz. Kilner/Mason
   jars, sterilized

MAKES 1 LITRE/QUART

Boil the beetroot in a pan of water until cooked through, 30–45 minutes, depending on their size. Drain, let cool a little and peel using your hands – the skin will come right off (disposable gloves can prevent staining).

Slice the beetroot into 5-mm/¼-inch slices and add to sterilized jars. Add the coarse salt on top.

Add the rest of the ingredients to a saucepan and bring to the boil to dissolve all the sugar completely. Leave to bubble for a minute or two, then take off the heat.

Pour the liquid over the beetroot to cover, then close the jars. Leave for at least 2 days before eating, but a week will be even better.

GOES WELL WITH *Meatballs, pork, pâté, salmon, avocado.*

AGURKESALAT
CUCUMBER & DILL QUICK PICKLE

All over Scandinavia, some form of pickled cucumber is used as a side for sandwiches, as a side to our famous meatballs – and, most importantly, as a topping on beloved hotdogs.

This agurkesalat is a real grandma recipe and can also be found alongside any smörgåsbord. It's simple to make, fresh in flavour and retains the crunch of the cucumber.

1 cucumber, thinly sliced
60 g/5 tablespoons caster/ superfine sugar
100 ml/⅓ cup white wine vinegar
1 tablespoon mustard seeds (optional)

2–3 tablespoons chopped dill, to taste
salt and freshly ground black pepper

500-ml/16-fl oz. Kilner/ Mason jar, very clean

MAKES 500 ML/16 FL OZ.

Put the cucumber slices on a plate and sprinkle a bit of salt over. Leave for 10–15 minutes.

In a saucepan, bring the sugar, vinegar, mustard seeds (if using) and 100 ml/⅓ cup water to a simmer. When the sugar has melted, take off the heat and season with salt and pepper.

Place the cucumber slices in a jar (discard any liquid that has been drawn out from salting). Top with the liquid and fresh dill and leave for at least an hour before eating.

Store for up to 1 week in the fridge.

TIP Seeing as this pickle is not made to be stored for a long time, you do not need to sterilize the jar before using. However, do make sure it is very clean.

GOES WELL WITH *Hotdogs, roast beef, roast pork, sausage, salami, meatballs, in salads and sandwiches.*

RÅSYLTEDE TOMATER
CHERRY TOMATO QUICKLE

These little gems go on many sandwiches and salads in our cafe. I find that cherry tomatoes are often a bit bland out of season, so this method of adding them to a vinegar solution without adding hot liquid means it brings out their flavour quickly and easily. This method is called 'raw pickling' but my wonderful chef friend Laura coined the term 'quickle', which sounds so much better – a sort of mix between a marinade and a pickle where the crunch of the veg or fruit is preserved. You need to store these in the fridge as they don't last that long.

300 g/10½ oz. cherry tomatoes
3 tablespoons honey
50 ml/3½ tablespoons white wine vinegar
50 ml/3½ tablespoons water

salt and freshly ground black pepper
a few thyme sprigs

500-ml/16-fl oz. Kilner/ Mason jar, very clean

MAKES 500 ML/16 FL OZ.

Halve the tomatoes and add to the jar. Add all the other ingredients and leave to marinate for at least an hour, ideally longer.

Store for 5–6 days in the fridge.

TIP Use on open sandwiches or in salads – this recipe will cover 10–12 open sandwiches, with leftovers.

VEGAN VERSION Replace the honey with maple syrup.

GOES WELL WITH *Roast beef, cauliflower, hot-smoked salmon... any sandwiches where you'd use tomatoes.*

RÅSYLTEDE RØDLØG, FENIKEL, GULEROD
RED ONION, CARROT OR FENNEL QUICKLE

Open sandwiches should evolve, and a good way to try something new is by experimenting with different pickles or quickles and vegetables.

This is an easy quickle – and the different vegetables liven up different sandwiches across the seasons.

200 ml/1 scant cup apple cider vinegar (for onion) or white wine vinegar (for fennel or carrot)

100 g/½ cup light brown soft sugar

1 bay leaf

10 peppercorns

a few sprigs of thyme or dill (optional)

500 g/1 lb. 2 oz. red onion, sliced
OR 1 fennel bulb, sliced
OR 3 carrots, sliced

1 teaspoon coarse salt

500-ml/16-fl oz. Kilner/Mason jar, very clean

MAKES 500 ML/16 FL OZ.

Add the vinegar, sugar, bay leaf, peppercorns and thyme or dill to a saucepan with 200 ml/1 scant cup water and bring to the boil. If making pickled onion, then cook the slices in the liquid for 1 minute first until soft (this removes some of the harshness of the onion that is hard to digest).

Add the sliced vegetables to the jar. Add the salt, then the hot liquid, so that it covers the vegetables, and close the lid.

Leave for at least 4 hours for the flavours to mingle – but try to leave for longer.

TIP As with all quickles, these they don't have a long shelf life (they last about 1 week), but they retain a good crunch.

GOES WELL WITH *Meatballs, egg, pâté. Great as extra toppings for both open and closed sandwiches.*

RÅSYLTEDE CHAMPIGNON
MUSHROOM QUICKLE

These mushrooms work as an alternative to pickled herring in vegetarian open sandwiches, but are also lovely as a simple sandwich topping. When replacing herring, I prefer the larger portobello mushrooms, as the pieces almost feel a bit like the fish. If you only have the smaller mushrooms, leave the pieces larger.

2 large portobello mushrooms (about 80 g/3 oz.), sliced.

40 g/3¼ tablespoons caster/superfine sugar

100 ml/⅓ cup white wine vinegar

½ teaspoon salt

a few peppercorns

500-ml/16-fl oz. Kilner/Mason jar, very clean

MAKES 500 ML/16 FL OZ.

Slice the mushrooms in large, long slices 3–4 cm/1¼–1½ inch thick.

Add all the ingredients, except the mushrooms, to a saucepan with 100 ml/⅓ cup water, and bring to a simmer. When the sugar has melted, take off the heat.

Place the mushroom slices in a jar. Top with the liquid, close firmly (turn the jar a few times to ensure they are all covered) and leave for at least an hour to cool down. Refrigerate overnight.

Store for 5 days in the fridge. To use, drain, then mix with your favourite 'herring' dressing (mustard, creamy or curry).

NOTE As this is a quick pickle that is made to be eaten not stored, you do not need to sterilize the jars before using. However, do make sure the jar is very clean.

GOES WELL WITH *Steak, chicken and pork and all veggie options.*

RØDLØGSKOMPOT
RED ONION RELISH

This makes a generous portion – too much for just a few open sandwiches, but it will keep for several weeks in the fridge. If you love caraway, you can add seeds to this relish for added oomph.

1 tablespoon neutral oil, such as sunflower oil

3 red onions, sliced

1 star anise

½ teaspoon salt

70 g/6 tablespoons light brown soft sugar

35 ml/2¼ tablespoons red wine vinegar

35 ml/2¼ tablespoons balsamic vinegar

½ tablespoon cornflour/cornstarch, dissolved in 2 tablespoons cold water

freshly ground black pepper

MAKES A GENEROUS AMOUNT

Heat the oil in a pan and sweat the onions with the star anise and salt over a medium heat for 10–15 minutes, stirring occasionally, until soft, but not yet coloured.

Add the sugar and vinegars and cook until the liquid has reduced by about two thirds (again, this will take 10–15 minutes).

Pour in the cornflour mixture and stir thoroughly. Cook for a further 2–3 minutes until the liquid has thickened.

Season with plenty of black pepper and, once cooled, adjust the salt if needed.

Store any leftovers in the fridge and use within 5 days.

GOES WELL WITH *Many sandwiches, but particularly well with beef, or on a cheeseboard or charcuterie board.*

REMOULADE
DANISH REMOULADE

Remoulade is a classic Danish sauce based on the French recipe, but it's not the same. Most people just buy it, but it's easy to make. Danes like to put remoulade on a lot of foods, from beef to fish.

50 g/1¾ oz. carrot

50 g/1¾ oz. cauliflower

50 g/1¾ oz. pickled gherkins

1 tablespoon capers

1 small shallot, chopped

150 ml/⅔ cup mayonnaise

100 ml/⅓ cup crème fraîche or sour cream

½ teaspoon medium curry powder

1 teaspoon turmeric (optional, mainly for colour)

½ teaspoon Dijon mustard

1 teaspoon white wine vinegar

2 tablespoons caster/superfine sugar

salt and freshly ground black pepper

MAKES ENOUGH FOR 5–7 LARGE SANDWICHES

Finely chop the carrots, cauliflower and pickled gherkins.

Mix all the ingredients together until well combined. I quite like a chunky remoulade, so I chop all the ingredients by hand; for a quicker result and smoother finish, you can pulse a few times in a food processor (but make sure it still has bits; it shouldn't be smooth).

Leave in the fridge for 30 minutes before using to allow the colour and flavour to develop.

Store any leftovers in the fridge and use within 5 days.

TIP Store-bought remoulade is very sweet – if you're used to this taste, add more sugar to taste.

GOES WELL WITH *Fried fish, breaded things, fries, cold roast beef, salami, meatballs, hotdogs.*

SALAD TOPPINGS

KARTOFFELSALAT
POTATO SALAD

This quick potato salad goes on the Danish meatball open sandwich in the café. It is easy to whip up with leftover cold potatoes and is super tasty.

This makes a generous portion (more than needed for open sandwiches), so if you're only making a few sandwiches, you can reduce the quantities or use the leftovers as a side dish.

1 tablespoon Dijon mustard

1 tablespoon capers

30 g/1 oz. pickled cucumber (use shop-bought or see Cucumber & Dill Quick Pickle, page 114), chopped

1 spring onion/scallion, thinly sliced (including the green bits)

3 tablespoons mayonnaise, or to taste

3 tablespoons Greek yogurt

1 tablespoon chopped chives

a small dollop of honey (optional)

200 g/7 oz. cold cooked waxy potatoes, cut into 5 mm–1-cm/⅛–½-inch squares

salt and freshly ground black pepper

MAKES ENOUGH FOR 3–4 SANDWICHES

Mix the ingredients, except the potatoes, together in a bowl and season. Add the potatoes and adjust the seasoning. If you prefer a creamier finish, add more mayonnaise.

Store any leftovers in the fridge and use within 5 days.

TIP This potato salad can be doubled in quantity for a main side – just cut the potatoes a bit bigger.

GOES WELL WITH *Meatballs (from any Scandinavian country) or as a side salad to most things.*

RÖDBETSALLAD
BEETROOT SALAD

This is the classic Swedish beetroot salad. At our café, we use this on many of our open sandwiches and also serve it as a side salad – it's very versatile. If you use pre-pickled beetroot (and let's face it, most of us do), try to find a brand that isn't too sweet or too sour.

300 g/10½ oz. pickled beetroot/beets (use shop-bought or see Pickled Beetroot, page 111), drained and cut into 5-mm/¼-inch pieces

1 tart apple, cut into 5-mm/¼-inch pieces

50 ml/3½ tablespoons mayonnaise, or to taste

50 ml/3½ tablespoons crème fraîche or sour cream, or to taste

a squeeze of lemon juice

a dash of balsamic vinegar

salt and freshly ground black pepper

1 tablespoon finely chopped chives, to serve (optional)

MAKES ENOUGH FOR 4 LARGE OR 8 SMALL SANDWICHES

Mix the pickled beetroot and apple in a bowl, add the mayonnaise, crème fraîche, lemon juice and balsamic vinegar, and stir. You want a good creamy consistency and a medium-pink colour (the beetroot should be drained properly to avoid a runny consistency).

Season to taste. Add more mayonnaise and crème fraîche if a creamier salad is desired.

Leave to set in the fridge for a few hours or even overnight. The colour will go a little darker, but if you prefer a lighter pink, just add a dollop of mayo or crème fraîche, just before serving.

It looks nice with finely chopped chives on top, to serve.

GOES WELL WITH *Meatballs, herring, egg, hot-smoked salmon, mackerel or as a smörgåsbord side.*

CRISPY TOPPINGS

RISTEDE LØG
CRISPY ONIONS

Many Scandinavian open sandwiches call for crispy onions. You can buy these ready made – most supermarkets stock these now, either in the salad section or the East Asian aisle (they're often used for sushi decoration). The homemade version is easy to make and gives a gourmet look.

1 white onion or 4 shallots
2–3 tablespoons plain/all-purpose flour (for gluten-free, swap with cornflour/cornstarch)
salt and freshly ground black pepper
150–200 ml/⅔–scant 1 cup vegetable oil, for frying

MAKES ENOUGH FOR 6–8 LARGE SANDWICHES

If you're using shallots, cut them into rings; if you're opting for a large onion, either keep in larger rings or cut it into quarters, then slice thinly.

Pop the flour, salt and pepper into a plastic bag, add the onions and shake until they are all coated. Discard the excess flour.

Heat the vegetable oil in a small saucepan to 140–150°C (285–300°F). If the temperature is too hot, the onions will burn; if it's too cold, they will go soggy.

Once the oil reaches frying temperature, test one onion ring to see how it cooks, then adjust the temperature as needed. When ready, add one-third of the onions to the oil and cook until golden brown. Remove with a slotted spoon and leave to drain on paper towels. Repeat with the other two batches.

The onions will crisp as they cool down. Store in an airtight container for up to 3 days.

GOES WELL WITH *Hotdogs, pâté, roast beef, salami, anything that has remoulade, meatballs.*

SPRØDT KYLLINGESKIND
CRISPY CHICKEN SKIN

This is one of those things from Denmark that I never knew I missed until I started making it. Now I've rediscovered it, I use it on everything – from open sandwiches to risotto. It adds a kick of oomph, umami and saltiness all in one.

skin from 8 chicken thighs/legs or 3–4 breasts
salt and freshly ground black pepper

MAKES ENOUGH FOR 10 LARGE SANDWICHES

Preheat the oven to 200°C (400°F) Gas 6.

Using a very sharp knife, scrape off any excess fat from the skin. Place the chicken skins as flat as you can on a lined baking sheet. You don't need oil for this. Season with salt and pepper.

Add a sheet of baking paper on top and weigh the skins down by adding another baking sheet on top. Place in the oven and bake for 15–20 minutes. For the last few minutes, remove the top baking sheet.

Once out of the oven, leave to cool. Cut or break into rough pieces before adding to open sandwiches.

Store in an airtight container for up to 5 days.

NOTE You can also use your air fryer to make these: on high heat, cook for 5–6 minutes and turn over and cook for the same amount of time again.

GOES WELL WITH *Everything! And can even be used as a base for canapés.*

GRØNSAGSCHIPS
VEGETABLE CRISPS

Using things such as vegetable chips is a good way to give a modern look when you decorate and serve your open sandwiches. You can vary with other vegetables as preferred.

1 parsnip OR 1 beetroot/beet OR 1 carrot OR 2–3 potatoes OR a mixture of all the above

1–2 tablespoons neutral oil, such as sunflower oil

salt

MAKES ENOUGH FOR 10 LARGE SANDWICHES

Preheat the oven to 150°C (300°F) Gas 2.

Using a mandoline (or some excellent skill with your knife or potato peeler), slice the vegetables into really thin slices, about 1–2 mm/1/16 inch thick. I like to do the carrots and beetroot in rounds, but I keep the parsnips long as they curl up slightly as they bake, which looks very nice.

Place in a bowl and add enough of the oil to coat all the slices, then transfer to a lined baking sheet, ensuring there's no overlapping.

Bake until crisped up. Parsnips cook more quickly than beetroot and carrot, so keep an eye and remove when crisp. You need 20–30 minutes for parsnips, a bit longer for carrots and potatoes and 40–60 minutes for beetroot. Lower the oven temperature if the vegetable crisps start to brown too quickly. Salt, if you want, while still warm.

Store in an airtight container and use within a few days.

NOTE You can also use your air fryer to make these (follow manufacturer's instructions). If you're not feeling like making these, bags of ready-made vegetable crisps and potato chips work fine on open sandwiches, too.

USE FOR *Beautiful decoration and crunch on open sandwiches, or as decoration for any dish.*

RISTEDE FRØ MED SOYA
STICKY SOYA SEEDS

These are not Scandi, but we use them at the café. A perfect open sandwich always has an element of crunch to it and while many traditional smørrebrød have raw onion rings or cucumber slices, this can both look and feel a little dated, so we use these seeds. Toast them just as they are – this is fine – or elevate them a bit with soy sauce.

50 g/6 tablespoons sunflower seeds

50 g/6 tablespoons pumpkin seeds

50 g/6 tablespoons white sesame seeds

25 g/3 tablespoons black sesame seeds

1 tablespoon light soy sauce

1 tablespoon honey (for vegan, replace with maple syrup)

1 tablespoon neutral oil, such as sunflower oil

MAKES 200 G/7 OZ.

Heat up a frying pan/skillet. Toast all the seeds in the pan for a few minutes, then add the liquids to the seeds. Toast and stir frequently until they start to caramelize.

Take off the heat and leave to cool. The seeds will stick together slightly in clusters.

Store in an airtight container and use within 14 days.

USE FOR *Adding extra crunch to everything, from open sandwiches to salads.*

COOKED & CURED TOPPINGS

GRAVAD LAX
DILL-CURED SALMON

Cured salmon is an essential part of food in Nordic countries. It isn't hard to cure your own salmon, it just takes time.

Invest in a good middle piece of salmon fillet, or even a whole side, and leave the skin on. The most important thing is the freshness and quality of the fish, as well as the balance of the curing ingredients used.

Dill is the traditional herb to use, but punchy flavours such as fennel and coriander also work. You might even want to try beetroot or even adding gin, vodka or aquavit.

I always freeze the salmon for 48 hours. Freezing kills most parasites, if any are present, so I think it's good practice to do this if you are unsure that this has been done before you've bought it.

1-kg/2¼-lb. piece of salmon fillet (middle bit, if available)

50 g/3½ tablespoons salt

80 g/6½ tablespoons white sugar

2 teaspoons white peppercorns, crushed

2 tablespoon gin, vodka or aquavit (optional)

2 bunches of dill (around 60 g/2 oz. in total)

MAKES 1 KG/2¼ LB (USE A SMALLER PIECE OF SALMON IF LESS IS REQUIRED)

Defrost the salmon in the fridge before using.

Once defrosted, check for bones by running very clean fingers across the fleshy side and using tweezers to pick out any stray bones you find. Cut the salmon across the middle into two equal pieces.

Mix together the salt, sugar and white peppercorns. Rub the alcohol (if using) and a bit of water over the fleshy sides, then rub in the salt, sugar and pepper. Ensure all the flesh is covered.

Chop the dill (including stems) and place on top of one of the pieces on the flesh side. Place the other piece on top, flesh-side down so the two sides are touching, and wrap the fish tightly in clingfilm/plastic wrap. Place the salmon in a plastic bag and transfer to the fridge. Turn the bag over several times a day for the following 2–3 days to ensure the cure is even. The salmon is ready when the colour of the flesh changes to slightly translucent.

Unwrap the fish and discard the herb filling (it's fine if some dill remains, but it should be mostly clear of rougher stalks).

Place the salmon skin-side down on a board and carve into thin slices, cutting through the fish with the knife held at a slight diagonal so that the skin is left behind.

The fish will keep for several days stored in the fridge.

GOES WELL WITH *Gravadlax sauce, new potatoes, beetroot/beets, egg and great in salads or part of a smörgåsbord buffet.*

FLÆSKESTEG
ROAST PORK

While many Scandinavians save the roast pork for the winter and Christmas time, many Danes will probably say it is their favourite meal and that it should be our national dish – we cook it all year round, serving it with boiled potatoes, gravy and red cabbage. It also happens to be excellent (and traditional) on open sandwiches, hence why I'm including it here.

1-kg/2¼-lb. piece of pork loin* (not rolled, but bone removed, fat left on and scored at 1-cm/ ½-inch intervals down to the meat, but without touching it)

2–3 bay leaves

5–6 whole cloves

salt and freshly ground black pepper

meat therometer

SERVES 3–4 PEOPLE FOR DINNER WITH ENOUGH LEFT OVER FOR OPEN SANDWICHES

* You can also use a fattier rib cut here rather than loin. This will produce a much fattier result but absolutely no less tasty – so If you prefer that, go for it.

Flæskesteg is most often made using pork loin, which has less fat than the belly cut and slices well for sandwiches the next day. We never separate the crackling from the meat while cooking, so leave it on.

Preheat the oven to 200°C (400°F) Gas 6.

Add just-boiled water to a roasting pan and place your pork, rind-side down, in the water. The water should be 1–1.5 cm/½ inch deep and just about cover the rind.

Place in the hot oven for 20 minutes, then pour out the water and turn the pork over. This initial stage will have separated the rind slices to help produce the crackling.

Pat the rind dry with paper towels, then salt liberally all over, ensuring plenty of coverage inside the cracks. Add the bay leaves and cloves to the roasting dish, along with 200 ml/1 scant cup water, then return to the oven, reducing the temperature to 130°C (275°F) Gas 1.

The pork will now need to roast for 1–2 hours until it reaches an internal temperature of 68°C (154°F). The roasting time completely depends on your oven and the size of the cut, so do keep checking the temperature with a meat thermometer.

Once the meat is just at the correct temperature, heat the grill/broiler, and place the pork underneath. Keep an eye on it – crackling burns easily so you may need to move it around under the heat until you have an even, crispy crackling. Use the meat thermometer to check that the temperature has risen above 72°C (162°F) in the thickest part of the meat at this stage.

Leave the pork to rest for at least 15 minutes before carving. Reserve the juices in the pan for gravy if you're enjoying the roast as a dinner.

GOES WELL WITH *All the pickles and quickles – from beetroot to cucumber, fennel, red cabbage and more.*

FRIKADELLER
DANISH MEATBALLS

There are as many recipes for Danish meatballs as there are families in Denmark, and they all taste slightly different. This is my mother Lena's recipe. Sometimes, she'd make them with just pork if veal wasn't available; adapt the recipe as you see fit. The secret to good frikadeller *is the amount of butter you fry them in, so don't be shy.*

300 g/10½ oz. minced/ground veal

200 g/7 oz. minced/ground pork (with a good fat content of around 15 per cent – don't go for a low-fat pork)

1 teaspoon salt

1 onion, grated

1 egg

50 g/1 scant cup dried breadcrumbs

1 tablespoon plain/all-purpose flour

a pinch of ground allspice (optional*)

a pinch of freshly grated nutmeg

100 ml/⅓ cup warm full-fat/whole milk with ½ beef or chicken stock/bouillon cube dissolved into it

100 ml/⅓ cup sparkling water

75 g/⅓ cup unsalted butter

a good glug of olive oil

freshly ground black pepper

MAKES 20 (ENOUGH FOR DINNER FOR 4)

* My mother never added the allspice. She would be upset that I told you that she did. I like allspice – but in her version, it's a no-go. Sorry Mum.

Place the minced meat and salt in a stand mixer with the paddle attachment. Mix for around 1 minute on medium speed.

Meanwhile, wrap the grated onion in a clean tea/dish towel and wring it shut to squeeze out any excess liquid. Add the onion to the meat and mix again, then add the egg, breadcrumbs, flour, allspice (if using), nutmeg, milk with dissolved stock cube and some black pepper. Mix until incorporated. Leave to rest in the fridge for at least 30 minutes.

Preheat the oven to 120°C (250°F) Gas ½.

Take the meat out of the fridge, then add the sparkling water and stir in.

Using a tablespoon, scoop out a quantity of meat mixture the size of a large egg. Use the flat of your (wet) hand to help shape the meatballs. Danish meatballs are not round, but slightly oval, similar to an egg – see the larger meatballs in the picture opposite.

In a frying pan/skillet, heat the butter and leave it to brown and bubble, then add a glug of oil. The quantity of butter is essential for these meatballs, or they just don't get the right crust and flavour.

Test one small meatball first just to make sure you have the right seasoning – and you can adjust and continue with the rest of the mixture. Fry the meatballs over a medium-high heat, in batches that allow plenty of room for turning, for 2–3 minutes on each side. Transfer to the warm oven to finish – and repeat until you have used all the meat.

These freeze well, but also keep for 3 days in the fridge.

GOES WELL WITH *Red cabbage, potato, beetroot/beets.*

KÖTTBULLAR
SWEDISH MEATBALLS

This recipe makes a family-sized portion of meatballs. It really doesn't pay to just make a quarter of a batch for a few sandwiches. You can freeze these and use them for dinner another day (served with mashed potato, lingonberry and creamy gravy, as is most traditional in Sweden).

50 g/1 scant cup fresh breadcrumbs
  (or porridge oats)

150 ml/⅔ cup warm meat stock
  (chicken works well, too)

1 tablespoon neutral oil, such as
  sunflower, plus extra for frying

1 onion, finely chopped

500 g/1 lb. 2 oz. minced/ground
  beef (minimum 10 per cent fat)

250 g/9 oz. minced/ground pork
  (minimum 10 per cent fat)

1 teaspoon salt

1 egg

2½ tablespoons plain/all purpose
  flour

1 teaspoon ground allspice

½ teaspoon ground black pepper

½ teaspoon ground white pepper

a dash of Worcestershire sauce
  or soy sauce

a knob/pat of unsalted butter

**SERVES 4 (OR 2 WITH PLENTY LEFT
OVER FOR OPEN SANDWICHES)**

Add the breadcrumbs to the warm stock and leave to soak while cooking the onion. Heat the oil in a frying pan/skillet, add the onion and fry over a low heat for 10–15 minutes.

Meanwhile, in a stand mixer (or by hand), add the meats and mix well with the salt. Add the egg, flour, spices, breadcrumbs, Worcestershire sauce and the cooked onion. Mix well. The mixture should be mouldable (if not, add a little more flour). Leave to rest in the fridge for 30 minutes.

Add a dash of oil and a generous knob of butter to the frying pan. Shape one meatball and cook it fully. Taste and check the final seasoning, adjusting if needed. Shape the meatballs into 2.5-cm/1-inch balls. Don't overcrowd the pan, as you need to be able to swirl the meatballs round to keep their shape. Cook in batches until done.

GOES WELL WITH *Beetroot Salad (see page 118), lingonberry, Remoulade (see page 117), beetroot and Crispy Onions (see page 120).*

BREADS

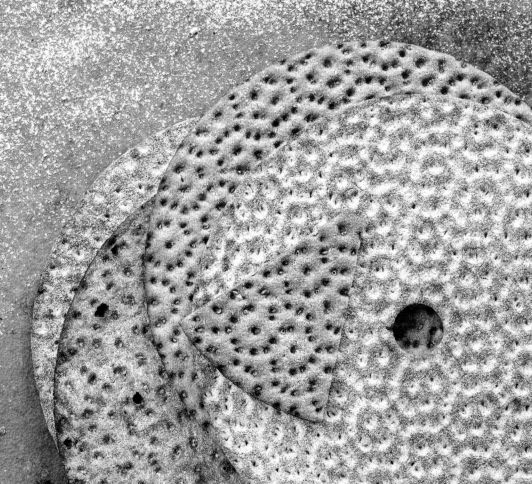

KLASSISK RUGBRØD
DANISH RYE BREAD

Every household in Denmark has a recipe for rye bread, usually with a long history to it. This one is from my little sister Ulla, who got it from her best friend, who got it from her mother, who got it from her aunt... and so the tradition carries on. If you don't have a sourdough starter, follow the instructions to make one from scratch. Read the recipe first – note that it will take over a week if you're making the starter from scratch.

DAY 1 INGREDIENTS
100 ml/⅓ cup water
100 g/1 scant cup rye flour

DAY 6 INGREDIENTS
4 tablespoons sourdough starter
150 ml/⅔ cup water
150 g/1 cup plus 2 tablespoons
  rye flour

DAY 7 INGREDIENTS
1 litre/4 cups lukewarm water
2 tablespoons salt
750 g/5⅓ cups dark rye flour
250 g/1¾ cups white strong/bread
  flour

DAY 8 INGREDIENTS
500 g/1 cup chopped rye kernels/
  rye grain
100 g/¾ cup sunflower seeds
100 g/¾ cup flaxseeds/linseeds
1 tablespoon dark syrup or dark
  corn syrup
2 tablespoons barley malt syrup
1 teaspoon barley malt powder
300 ml/1¼ cups lukewarm water
  or malt beer

*1.8-kg/4-lb. traditional rye bread
  pan, greased and lined (or split
  the dough between 2 loaf pans
  and adjust the time accordingly,
  using a thermometer to check
  it is baked)*

MAKES 1 LOAF

DAYS 1–6 (MAKING A STARTER) Mix the Day 1 ingredients together and leave in tub on the kitchen counter, lightly covered. Stir daily. Within 4–5 days, it will start to bubble. On Day 6, add the Day 6 ingredients to the starter and stir with a non-metal spoon. Leave for another 12–18 hours and the starter should be ready to use (you should see some serious bubbling action – if not, wait a bit longer).

DAY 7 Take 300 ml/1¼ cups of the starter (discarding any leftover starter) and mix it with the Day 7 ingredients. Leave in a bowl on your kitchen counter, covered with clingfilm/plastic wrap, for 24 hours.

DAY 8 Remove 300 ml/1¼ cups of the dough and place in a tub in the fridge for the next time you bake (this is your starter going forward). Mix the rest of the dough with the Day 8 ingredients in a stand mixer on low speed for around 10 minutes. The dough will be sticky and gloopy, like a thick oatmeal porridge.

Grease and line the rye bread pan. Fill the pan no more than three-quarters full, cover with clingfilm/plastic wrap and leave for another 8 hours on the kitchen table.

Preheat the oven to its hottest setting, around 250°C (475°F) Gas 9.

With a fork, prick the top of the rye bread all over. Brush with water and pop into the oven, immediately turning it down to 180°C (350°F) Gas 4. Bake for 1–1½ hours, or until the internal temperature reaches 98°C (208°F) – the baking time will vary depending on your pan and oven.

Remove the loaf from the pan and cover with a damp tea/dish towel to ensure that a very hard crust does not form as it cools.

Store in a plastic bag to keep the loaf soft. Leave for another 24 hours before eating as the bread needs to settle.

NOTE Feed your starter in the fridge: once or twice a week, add a few spoonfuls of rye flour and an equal quantity of water to keep it alive. When you want to bake more, start from Day 7 again.

SÖTLIMPA
SWEDISH SWEET LOAF

Swedes mostly eat crispbread, but they also love sweetened breads like this one.
The end result isn't as sweet as you'd expect, but the sugars are important for taste
and texture, as well as the proving. I adore this bread almost straight out of the
oven with a good strong cheese. This recipe makes two large loaves, but if you
wish to make three smaller ones, reduce your baking time accordingly. If proving
overnight, you can reduce the yeast by at least half and leave, covered, to rise in a
room at 12–14°C (54–57°F) for 12 hours. You can bake this bread in pans or free-hand.

50 g/1¾ oz. fresh yeast

100 g/½ cup dark brown soft sugar

75 g/¼ cup golden/corn syrup

50 g/3½ tablespoons unsalted butter, melted and cooled slightly

100 ml/⅓ cup soured dairy product, such as buttermilk

450 g/3¼ cups white strong bread flour, plus extra for dusting

400 g/scant 4 cups white rye flour

100 g/¾ cup wholemeal/whole-wheat rye flour

1 heaped teaspoon salt

1 egg, beaten

neutral oil, such as sunflower oil (or a beaten egg), for brushing

MAKES 2 LOAVES

In a stand mixer, add the fresh yeast and 500 ml/2 cups lukewarm water (no warmer than 37°C/98°F), and stir to dissolve for a minute or so. Add the sugar and syrup and keep mixing for another minute or so, then add the melted butter and soured dairy product. Start adding the flour bit by bit, along with the salt and egg.

Keep adding the flour and knead the dough for around 5 minutes. The dough should be stretchy, but not dry. You may not need all the flour, so reserve any remainder for the second kneading.

Cover the bowl with clingfilm/plastic wrap and leave to rise in a warm place for about an hour until the dough has doubled in size.

Turn out onto a floured surface and knead the dough with your hands for a few minutes. Cut into two pieces, then shape into loaves or place in loaf pans. Leave to rise again for 40 minutes.

Preheat the oven to 220°C (425°F) Gas 7.

Brush the surface of the loaves with oil (or beaten egg) or oil. Place in the preheated oven, then immediately reduce the heat to 200°C (400°F) Gas 6. The baking time is around 30–40 minutes, or until baked through. Watch the surface of the bread – if it goes brown too quickly, reduce the heat a little.

Remove from the oven, cover with a damp tea/dish towel to prevent a crust forming and leave to cool.

RUGBRØD
SEEDED RYE BREAD

Almost all dark rye bread sold in Scandinavian bakeries is made with a sourdough. It gives depth, flavour and structure. Sometimes, however, you just need rye bread and don't have a sourdough because you killed it by being neglectful (yes, I do that). This is a good back-up rye bread loaf, which is ready in a few hours, rather than several days.

200 g/1 generous cup cracked rye kernels (see tip)

1 teaspoon lemon juice

200 ml/1 scant cup full-fat/whole milk, at room temperature

15 g/½ oz. fresh yeast

1 tablespoon dark molasses or black treacle

200 ml/1 scant cup Guinness or other stout

150 g/1½ scant cups wholegrain/whole-wheat rye flour

300g white bread flour

100 g/¾ cup sunflower seed

50 g/6 tablespoons pumpkin seeds, plus extra for topping

75 g/ flaxseed/linseed

1 tablespoon fine salt

1.35-kg/3-lb. loaf pan, greased and lined

MAKES 1 LOAF

NOTE This recipe, in a 1.35-kg/3-lb. pan, will make slightly smaller slices than the classic Danish Rye Bread (see page 130). If you prefer larger slices, use a slightly bigger pan but amend the baking time accordingly (use a thermometer to check the internal temperature).

Add the cracked rye to a bowl and top with 200 ml/1 scant cup hot water. Leave until the rye has absorbed the water and the mixture is lukewarm for around 30 minutes.

Add the lemon juice to the milk and leave for 15 minutes to curdle. Soured milk works best here (because there is no sourdough in this bread, you need something sour).

Add the fresh yeast to a stand mixer and then add 150 ml/⅔ cup lukewarm water and allow to dissolve. Add all other ingredients (salt last) and mix well for 4–5 minutes in the stand mixer, then cover with a damp tea/dish towel and leave to rise for about an hour. It will look gloopy and porridge-like.

Using a spoon, beat the air out of the mixture. Pour into the loaf pan, cover and leave to rise again for another hour (you can also leave to rise in the fridge overnight instead – if you plan on doing so, you can reduce the amount of yeast by half). It will not rise a lot, maybe only by a quarter.

Preheat the oven to 220°C (425°F) Gas 7.

With a fork, prick the top of the rye bread all over, 2.5 cm/1 inch below the surface, to keep the bread level when baking and avoid the air pockets. Sprinkle the seeds all over the top. Brush with water and pop into the oven, immediately turning it down to 180°C (350°F) Gas 4. Bake for 1 hour, or until the internal temperature reaches 98°C (208°F).

Rye bread is always sticky when just baked. For best results, wrap in clingfilm/plastic wrap and wait for 24 hours before eating, or at least until it has cooled down completely.

You can freeze this bread (but it does last a good 3–5 days after baking).

TIP If you cannot get hold of cracked rye, use whole rye pulsed in a food processor. It's not quite the same, but is a good substitute. Never use whole rye – the seed needs to be cut or the liquid will not be absorbed.

FRANSKBRØD MED KOMMEN
CARAWAY LOAF

Mormor *means 'grandmother' across Scandinavia. My* mormor's *house always had a faint scent of caraway –* my morfar *(grandfather) was a famous cheesemaker and his speciality was a young soft cheese smoked over nettles and hay and topped with caraway seeds. This easy caraway loaf reminds me of her house and all the lovely cheeses we used to eat there.*

25 g/1 oz. fresh yeast or 13 g/
   2½ teaspoons active dry yeast

250 ml/1 cup buttermilk, at room
   temperature

1 tablespoon sugar

1 teaspoon salt

2 teaspoons caraway seeds,
   plus extra for topping

1 teaspoon fennel seeds,
   lightly crushed

300 g/2 cups wholegrain spelt flour

150–200 g/1–1½ cups strong white
   bread flour, plus extra for dusting

beaten egg, for brushing

*450-g/1-lb. loaf pan, greased
   and lined*

MAKES 1 LOAF

If using fresh yeast, add it to 150 ml/⅔ cup lukewarm water and stir until dissolved. If using active dry yeast, pour 150 ml/⅔ cup lukewarm water into a bowl, sprinkle on the yeast and whisk together. Cover with clingfilm/plastic wrap and leave in a warm place for about 15 minutes to activate and become frothy and bubbly.

Pour the yeast mixture into a large bowl. Add the buttermilk and sugar, then the salt and stir well. Add the caraway seeds and fennel seeds. Add the mixture to a stand mixer with a dough hook attached, and start adding the spelt flour, bit by bit, while mixing on a low setting. Keep adding until all the spelt flour has been kneaded in, then start adding the strong white bread flour, also bit by bit. You may or may not need all of it (or you may need a bit more), depending on the strength of your flour. Knead on low speed for 7–8 minutes until the dough is elastic and firm, but not dry.

Place the dough in a bowl, cover with clingfilm/plastic wrap and leave to rise for at least 30 minutes until doubled in size. Turn out onto a surface dusted with flour, knead by hand and shape into a loaf to fit into the pan.

Place the dough into the loaf pan. Score the dough 4–5 times along the top and leave to rise for a further 30 minutes.

Preheat the oven to 200°C (400°F) Gas 6.

Brush the tops of the loaf with egg and add a scattering of caraway seeds. Bake for 30 minutes in the preheated oven or until well risen and golden brown in colour.

NOTE I usually place an ovenproof bowl of water in the bottom of the oven during baking to ensure a good crust.

FRANSKBRØD
WHITE LOAF WITH POPPYSEED

Go into any Danish traditional bakery and you will see this white loaf. The name translates as 'French bread' and it is the standard of all the loaves. I've not included it in any of my books until now because I always favoured artisan bread, the fancier loaves. However, when I go to Denmark and I want to make a real traditional open sandwich that calls for white bread, no other loaf will do.

You can cold-rise this dough in the fridge overnight. If you do, reduce the yeast by half and let it come to room temperature before continuing the recipe.

650 ml/2¾ cups full-fat/whole milk

25 g/1 oz. fresh yeast

1 generous tablespoon honey or sugar

1 kg/7 cups strong white bread flour, plus extra for dusting

50 g/3½ tablespoons butter, softened

1 generous teaspoon fine salt (if using flakes, you need more)

beaten egg or milk, for brushing

poppy seeds, for topping

2 x 1.35-kg/3-lb. loaf pans, greased and lined, or a large baking sheet, lined

MAKES 2 LOAVES

Heat the milk to 32–35°C (90–95°F), then add to a stand mixer. Add the yeast and stir, then add the honey. Once dissolved, start adding the flour, bit by bit, followed by the softened butter (it will mix in). Add the salt and keep kneading until you have a uniform dough for about 5 minutes.

Place the dough in a bowl, cover with clingfilm/plastic wrap and leave to rise until doubled in size – this will depend on how warm your kitchen is. It is usually takes about 1–1½ hours, but time matters less than the size of the rise. I don't use a full quantity of yeast in this recipe to avoid the over yeasted aftertaste that comes from using too much.

Turn the dough out onto a floured surface and knock it back (lightly punch the dough to expel any air). Split into two pieces, and shape into loaves. If using loaf pans, add the dough, smoothest side up. Otherwise, place on a lined baking sheet, ensuring they are not too close together. Cover and leave to rise for another 30–40 minutes.

Preheat the oven to 220°C (425°F) Gas 7 and place an ovenproof bowl of water in the bottom of the oven to help create steam.

Just before you pop the bread in the oven, brush with beaten egg or milk, and dust a generous amount of poppy seeds on top.

If you're using tins, score each dough once down the middle lengthways. If not, then score each dough several times at an angle.

Pop into the oven and cook for 5 minutes on full heat, then turn it down to 180°C (350°F) Gas 4 for another 25 minutes, or until the internal temperature is 92°C (198°F).

GOES WELL WITH *We use white bread for fish and seafood sandwiches, mainly – but it's also great with Beetroot Salad (see page 118) and Swedish Meatballs (see page 127). This is also great toasted or just fresh with butter.*

KNÄCKEBRÖD
CRISPBREAD

In Scandinavia, crispbread is not a diet bread – it just happens to be healthy and delicious. It has been a staple on our lunch tables since Harald Bluetooth was a nipper. Enjoy with sliced meats, pâtés, smoked fish or grated Västerbotten cheese mixed with crème fraîche and cream cheese, spiked with extra pepper and topped with cloudberry jam/jelly.

25 g/1 oz. fresh yeast or 13 g/2½ teaspoons dried/active dry yeast*

250 ml/1 cup lukewarm milk

2 tablespoons runny honey OR bread syrup OR golden/corn syrup

150 g/1 cup wholemeal/wholegrain rye flour

300–400 g/2¼–3 cups light rye flour

2 teaspoons salt

50–75 g/¼–½ cup seeds, spices or toppings of your choice (I sometimes use pumpkin seeds, poppy seeds or sunflower seeds; for stronger flavours, I use cumin, caraway or fennel seeds. You can even add ground cinnamon for a festive feel)

2–4 large baking sheets, greased and lined with baking parchment or a large pizza stone

MAKES 8 LARGE OR 16 SMALL

* You can also make this with a sourdough starter, but you'll need to try with your own starter to see what quantity works for you.

If using fresh yeast, add the yeast and warm milk to a stand mixer with a dough hook attached. Mix until the yeast has dissolved. If using dried/active dry yeast, pour the warm milk into a bowl, sprinkle over the yeast and whisk together. Cover with clingfilm/plastic wrap and leave in a warm place for about 15 minutes to activate and become frothy and bubbly. Pour into the mixer with a dough hook attached.

Add the honey or syrup and stir again. Sift together the flours and salt and add 350 g/2½ cups to the mixer to start with. Continue to mix with the dough hook for at least 5 minutes on medium speed. The dough needs to be firm but if it is too dry and crumbly, then mix in a few tablespoons of water, or if it's too sticky, add the remaining flour.

Cover the bowl with clingfilm/plastic wrap and leave the dough to rest for around an hour in a warm place. It will not rise too much, but should puff up a little.

Preheat the oven to 220°C (425°F) Gas 7. Add a pizza stone to the oven if you have one handy (this speeds up the cooking).

Turn the dough out onto a lightly floured surface and gently knead it through. Split into 8 large or 16 smaller pieces. Roll each piece of dough into a ball, then roll out each onto a piece of baking parchment until really thin or around a millimetre in thickness. Arrange on the baking sheets. Add your chosen seeds or toppings, pushing them into the dough slightly. Brush with water and prick liberally with a fork all over. I like my crispbread salty, so I usually also add a sprinkle of salt flakes at this stage too. I also usually cut a hole in the middle of mine, but this is just for show. If preparing in batches, keep the dough covered with a kitchen cloth to prevent it from drying out.

Bake in the preheated oven for 4–8 minutes or until slightly browned and firm. If you are not using a pizza stone, you may need to turn the crispbread over midway through cooking.

Remove from the oven and allow to cool on the trays. Once the oven has cooled to just warm, pop the crispbread back in to finish drying.

HÖNÖKAKOR
SWEDISH RYE FLAT BREADS

The Swedish hönökaka *is named after the island of Hönö off the coast of Gothenburg, where it was originally baked by fishing and farming families. Shop-bought* hönökakor *are common in Sweden, but can be a bit sweet. I use light brown sugar, but not as much as in other recipes – I find it gives a rounded taste to the bread. I make a few of these weekly for the kids' lunchboxes and as a bread for a smörgåsbord. It also goes really well as a sandwich bread with fish and seafood. I prefer a plain* hönökaka, *but you can add fennel or caraway seeds, or whatever else you might like.*

50 g/2 oz. fresh yeast
50 g/¼ cup light brown soft sugar
400 g/4 scant cups white rye flour
400 g/3 cups white strong bread
  flour, plus extra for dusting
  (you may not use all of either flour,
  so use them equally as you go)
1 tablespoon salt
100 g/7 tablespoons butter,
  at room temperature

**MAKES 6 LARGE BREADS
(THEY FREEZE REALLY WELL)**

Dissolve the fresh yeast in 500 ml/2 cups lukewarm water in the bowl of a stand mixer. Mix for a minute or so, then add the sugar and mix again to dissolve. Add two-thirds of each of the two flours, plus all the salt, and start mixing. You may not need all the flour, which is why you start with the amount indicated, then add more of each as you need it. Add the butter and keep mixing until it is incorporated. Add more of the flours as needed. When the dough starts letting go of the sides of the bowl (after around 5 minutes of kneading in the machine and with enough flour added), cover the dough and leave to rest in a warm place for around an hour, or until it has doubled in size.

Turn the dough out onto a floured surface and knead, then cut it into six equal-sized pieces. Roll each one out to a circle with a diameter of 30 cm/12 inches, then prick all over with a fork and place on baking parchment. Leave to rise again under a tea/dish towel for around 40 minutes.

Preheat the oven to 240°C (475°F) Gas 9. I add the baking sheets to the oven at this stage, as placing the *hönökakor* on a hot sheet speeds up the baking on the underside of the bread – much the same as using a pizza stone to make a base.

Prick again with the fork just before you pop the bread into the oven (you may need to bake them in batches). Bake for around 8 minutes, but keep an eye on them, as they can go brown quickly due to the sugar content. You want them slightly golden, but not overly brown.

Remove from the oven and leave to cool under a damp tea/dish towel while you bake the rest of the breads.

INDEX

ACKNOWLEDGEMENTS

Thank you to the wonderful team who worked on this book:

Julia Charles, Megan Smith, Leslie Harrington, Abi Waters, Patricia Harrington, Kate Reeves-Brown, Peter Cassidy, Tony Hutchinson, Kathy Kordalis and Riina Salmela.

Thank you so much to my agent, Jane Graham-Maw, without whom I would never have been brave enough to start writing again.

To our brilliant team at ScandiKitchen: Freja Haulrik, Emma Uimonen, Maria Szabo, Sini Muuronen, Ricky Palmer, Olga Glebaite, Mia Gursoy, Amanda Batista, Eliza Robertson, Sujith Sujith, Annie Calwell, Caterina Schifaudo, Daria Saleh, Emeliina Vilo, Ida Tollbo, Saara Simmons, Katalin Buzle, Imogen Vowles, Amalie Linderman, Rebeca Bejan, Vivek Patel, Myo Thant, Alicja Balczus, Paul Ionita, Annastiina Peltola, George Caminata, Chun Hang Sit, Krupali Piyushkumar, Majka Loevendahl, Nadia Lundquist and Marcus Blomgren.

Peter Mölker, David Cross, David Holberton and Chris Wright, for keeping us in line.

An extra special thanks to the wonderful Riina Salmela who heads up our café: for all her hard work assisting with this book, from testing to research, styling on the shoot, and so much more.

Thank you, David Kronholm Jørgensen, for your ever watchful eye.

And above all, for Jonas, Astrid and Elsa, with all my love always.